The Radiance of the Inner Splendor

THE RADIANCE
OF

THE INNER SPLENDOR

LLOYD JOHN OGILVIE

THE UPPER ROOM
Nashville, Tennessee

THE RADIANCE OF THE INNER SPLENDOR

Lines from the poem "Credo" by John Oxenham are used by permission of T. Dunkerly.

The scripture quotations not otherwise identified are from the Revised Standard Version of the Bible, copyrighted 1946, 1952 and © 1971 by the Division of Christian Education, National Council of the Churches of Christ in the United States of America, and are used by permission. • The initials KJV are used throughout this book to identify quotations from the King James Version of the Bible. • Quotations from *The New English Bible,* © The Delegates of the Oxford University Press and the Syndics of the Cambridge University Press 1961 and 1970, are reprinted by permission. The initials NEB are used to identify *New English Bible* quotations. • Quotations from *The New Testament in Modern English,* by J. B. Phillips, are reprinted with permission of the Macmillan Company. Copyright © 1958 by J. B. Phillips. • Quotations from the *Good News Bible, The Bible in Today's English Version* (TEV), copyright by American Bible Society 1966, 1971, © 1976, are used by permission. • Quotations noted with the initials TLB are from *The Living Bible,* copyright © 1971 by Tyndale House Publishers. • Scripture quotations designated NASB are from the *New American Standard Bible,* © The Lockman Foundation 1960, 1962, 1963, 1968, 1971. • The scripture quotations designated NKJB-NT in this publication are from *The New King James Bible—New Testament.* Copyright © 1979, Thomas Nelson, Inc., Publishers. Used by permission of the publisher.

Book design by Harriette Bateman
Cover transparency by John Netherton

Second Printing: March 1982 (5)

Library of Congress Catalog Card No.: 80-51524

ISBN 0-8358-0405-4

PRINTED IN THE UNITED STATES OF AMERICA

To George Phelps,
whose vision and generosity model two great truths:

You can't outgive God;
what he guides, he provides.

Contents

Foreword

IF YOU NEED a gracious, grace-filled word, here it is.

In his letter to the *Colossians,* Paul has a section on how Christians should relate to other persons (3:18; 4:6). In these practical instructions he focuses on several kinds of relationships—especially relationships within the family and between Christians and non-Christians. His instructions for Christian-with-outsider relationships provide special guidance for personal evangelism, but are relevant to all our relationships.

After admonishing us to be motivated by prayer, to be wise in our behavior toward non-Christians, to redeem the time by being alive to every opportunity to witness, Paul adds a challenging word: *Let your speech always be gracious, seasoned with salt* (Colossians 4:6). What marvelous wisdom!

Lloyd John Ogilvie has appropriated that wisdom.

His speech, verbal and written, is an expression of grace "seasoned with salt."

Dr. Ogilvie is one of the most attractive, compelling, exciting preachers in America today. At First Presbyterian Church in Hollywood, California, Sunday after Sunday, crowds "hear him gladly." At conferences, retreats, seminars, and preaching missions throughout the United States for which he is in constant demand, people listen and respond with grateful hearts.

He is as exciting a writer as he is a preacher. This is so because he takes writing and preaching seriously, and has in both the same aim—to share the gospel in as compelling a way as possible. He has a passion for sharing the Good News of Jesus Christ, and he pays the price of long hours of study, prayer, reflection, writing, and rewriting which are required for the message to be communicated effectively.

His preaching and writing is rooted in scripture, but is marked by that rare gift of personal application. "That's for me, what I need, where I am," is the response we make to his word. He is confessional, not only in the sense of sharing the pain and failure of his own life, but confessional in the sense of his faith and strength that he has found in Christ.

Paul said our speech should be flavored with salt. That means at least this: It should be *earthy*, reflecting what goes on in all our lives and teaching our most fundamental feelings, needs, hopes, failures, dreams. This book is a witness to the fact that Lloyd Ogilvie's writings are salty—earthy in that they meet us where we are. *Grace*, as Paul used it in giving instruction for our speech, has two meanings. It has to do with *charm*—attractiveness. It also has to do with gift, the gift of God's love. Both these meanings are appropriate in describing

10

Lloyd Ogilvie's words. They are gracious, attractive, and charming in that they are not only interesting but also compelling. They are grace-filled. They are a channel through which God's gift of himself in Jesus Christ can come to us. This is especially meaningful in relation to the theme of this book, *the fruit of the Spirit*. You will discover here a fresh and challenging presentation of the exciting possibility of being fruitful, creative, powerful, and redemptive because you are in Christ. The expression of his Spirit can grow in you, and through you, and from you.

So I conclude the way I began. If you need a gracious, grace-filled word, here it is, and it has flavor, the unique flavor of a person who has been with Christ and shares his grace.

MAXIE D. DUNNAM
WORLD EDITOR
THE UPPER ROOM

11

Introduction

THERE IS A figure of speech in the New Testament that has an agrarian, almost archaic sound. It seems strangely out of sync in vocabularies of Christians living at the edge of the twenty-first century—in a technological society where one branch of science is preparing us for life in the galaxies, and another moves closer to producing a disease-free race of "ideal" human beings by means of the precise manipulation of human genes.

The figure of speech I refer to is "fruit of the Spirit." Far from being obsolete, the idea captured in this image resembles and yet transcends the temporal promises of the technologies I have just mentioned as a candle flame is transcended by the sun!

"Fruit of the Spirit" is the code name the apostle Paul uses for the spiritual "transplant" that takes place when the nature of Christ is formed and begins to grow in men and women destined to live beyond time and space in resurrected bodies. It is also the recurring theme of this book.

Just because you have been graced with God's forgiveness, it does not necessarily follow that the fruit of the Spirit is actively developing in you. Not only was I a Christian, but I was a clergyman for eight years before I understood the personal implications of the Holy Spirit. The truth is this: Because the Holy Spirit does dwell within you, a new kind of action on your part is now possible. But it is not automatic.

It seems incredible that I had not fully appreciated that the steps in becoming a Christian climaxed in the indwelling power of the Holy Spirit. Humankind's need, God's action, the commitment of one's life to Christ— that was as far as it went. But that leaves out the liberating experience of Christianity—the magnificent culmination of God's generosity. The power dimension is in the fruit of the Spirit, coming as a result of Christ in us and making us like himself.

It is absolutely impossible to live within our own strength the kind of life Christ has called us to live. No amount of culture, education, or effort on our part that is not empowered by the spirit of God can produce Christian character.

There is nothing more tragic than a vision without the power to live it and nothing more debilitating than the discovery that the demands of becoming a vital Christian are too much for this genetic combination we call "self." We end up being inauthentic people, prisoners of the falseness that results when the word *Christian* becomes an adjective for a self-conscious life-style instead of the source of a divine life force.

There is nothing more demeaning for most people than being apprehended every Sunday from the pulpit and charged with the crime of not loving enough, not being gentle or kind enough, not suffering long enough, without having our rights read to us—God only requires *from* us what he places *in* us.

"Every time we say, 'I believe in the Holy Spirit,' " J. B. Phillips said, "we mean that we believe that there is a living God able and willing to enter human personality and change it."

And so say I.

The implications behind Paul's code name are radical. They are also profoundly personal. Would you like to experience the deep energy of pure joy? Could the parched quality of your life be replenished with the soft dew of peace? Do you need to suffer long in some relationship? There is auxiliary power for all of that and more. There is new control power to arrest the countdown for those debilitating emotional blast-offs, new courage to risk gentleness without fear of being exploited, reinforcement for diminishing self-control.

But wait, do you *want* a new personality?

Is it possible that you have developed a spiritual narcissism—a fascination with what has been your experience that will keep you from fresh experiences of God's grace? Putting it another way, are you more committed to the God of your experience than the fresh experience of God? The reason so many Christians find that they have such grave difficulty with their own human nature is that the fruit of the Spirit has not penetrated into the flesh nature of their humanity.

We are going to examine the attributes of this new personality power as Paul listed them for the Galatian Christians:

The fruit of the Spirit is love, joy, peace, patience, kindness, goodness, faithfulness, gentleness, self-control.

GALATIANS 5:22-23

There is a slight variance in the way these characteristics are translated in different texts, but the essence remains constant.

How did Paul choose this amazing symbol? Did it come in a flash of inspiration, or did he reflect long and hard before he selected the word *fruit* from ordinary language as a symbol for this hidden life force? In any case, the choice is not out of character with the way he thought and taught. He coined the phrase "eyes of the heart" as a takeoff from eyes of the body, why not a progression from fruit of the body to "fruit of the spirit"? Inasmuch as we bring new physical life into the world through birth, we can release new spiritual life by rebirth, Paul seems to be saying.

If we have been brought up in the church, some of us will find it a good exercise to avoid any association of the fruit of the Spirit with visual aids such as melons, apples, or pears. Paul's code word concerns itself primarily with the *process* of growth. Whether deep in the soil, in the soft, silent womb, or deep in the human spirit, all new births have something in common. Each is intricately programmed for growth, but all require the cooperation of forces and environments outside themselves to reach their potential. And so does the miraculous growth process of the fruit of the Spirit.

You will not encounter many theological words or phrases in this book, but that is not to say that its theological implications are not profound. The impact of the fruit of the Spirit for our personalities, our character,

16

and our relationships with others is expressed here without apology in incarnational language. And there is a good precedent for that. The Word, the ultimate truth about God and what it means to be his person, became flesh. He became a son with parents to honor, sisters to protect, younger siblings to deal with. Later, he had to find a home for an aging mother. He also had a few friends with questionable associations to whom he was loyal.

In a world without penicillin, air conditioning, and modern plumbing, God's Son met human demands head-on and fleshed out in the simple graces of love, joy, peace, patience, kindness, goodness, faithfulness, gentleness, and self-control. And it was in observing the quality of these earthly, everyday relationships with the people of his world that John made this profound theological affirmation: "The Word was made flesh, and dwelt among us, (and we beheld his glory, the glory as of the only begotten of the Father,) full of grace and truth" (John 1:14, KJV).

This book is about the continuing life of Jesus Christ in you and me. I invite you to do more than read it. Experience it. Let the world see once again a fraction of that radiance of inner splendor.

I am deeply indebted to Mary Tregenza for transcribing the tapes of a series of messages I gave on the "Fruit of the Spirit" and for working closely with me on the development of the content for the book. Her friendship and expertise are a source of joy. My assistant, Jeri Gonzalez, has been a wonderful help in the typing of the final manuscript for publication. Her enthusiasm for the project spurred me on to completion.

1
The First Half

I HAD BEEN a Christian and a pastor for several years before I discovered the inner splendor—life in all its fullness. My conversion in college gave me a firm conviction of Jesus Christ as my Savior and Lord. Seeking to follow Christ, I finished college, seminary, and graduate school.

The scriptures were my constant companion. I preached and taught with every fiber of my being. The Lord was gracious, and many around me experienced his love and forgiveness and started the high adventure of discipleship in the twentieth century.

It was during the second year of my first full-time parish in Winnetka, Illinois, that I realized that something was terribly wrong. Something was missing inside me.

The excitement of my conversion and the intellectual investigation of the faith had carried me along in a rushing river of enthusiasm. The exterior of my life was highly polished with Christian behavior. My vocabulary was punctuated with carefully worded truth and insight. In terms of large congregations, new buildings, and expanding budgets, my ministry would have been considered successful.

Inside I was empty.

I grew strangely insecure, anxious, and fearful. The old problem of self-esteem, battled in adolescence, reared its ugly, fiendish head and pressed me to work all the harder to assure success.

The approbation and affirmation of people became a narcotic to which I was becoming addicted, so I sharpened my human talents to ensure a steady supply of both. And when the talent ran out, a great deal of manipulation masquerading as motivation was used.

Do you have any idea what I am talking about?

Two factors brought my inner emptiness to crisis proportions. One occurred in my marriage. For all my study of the scriptures, I realized the one thing I could not do was love unselfishly. I kept tripping over the perpendicular pronoun each time I tried to love my wife in actions and language significant and satisfying to her.

The other cause of alarm was in my ministry. Many persons who had become Christians under my leadership were facing serious problems living out the implications of the gospel in their relationships. Their theology was impeccable. Their verbal witness was solidly evangelical. Their churchmanship was admirable. But, like their pastor, they were trying to be Christians in their own strength.

It was then I was forced to face one of the most disturbing truths about leadership—we can lead others only so far as we have gone ourselves. Nothing can happen through us which has not happened to us. Obviously, what my people needed had not happened to me.

The Lord had allowed the crisis to bring me to the astounding realization that I was living with only half a blessing. During the solitude and quiet of a study leave, as I was preparing the next year's sermons, my prayers for my people forced me to admit that I had preached only half the gospel.

Certainly I had preached Christ as the crucified and resurrected Lord of all life. My sermons were packed with what Christ had done for us, or what he could do with us as our companion and friend. But inadvertently I had avoided his promise of what he could do *in* us. I fell to my knees and asked for help.

I will never forget what happened. As I resumed my study, I was guided to John 10:10. Christ's words exploded with a freshness. It was as if I had never heard him before:

I am come that they might have life, and that they might have it more abundantly.

What thundered with clarity was that I had just read a two-dimensional promise—first life, and then abundant life. The first part dealt with what the Lord came to do. The second part dealt with what he comes to do now.

Suddenly I was face to face with the truth implicit in Paul's code name. It was a truth I had never dealt with before. I had preached the life of Christ and taught that the Christian life was the identification with Christ's cross for our forgiveness, his resurrection for our victory over death, and his living presence for the guidance of

21

our daily lives. Now the Lord seemed to be saying, "That's only half the blessing. Press on!"

I checked the meaning of *abundant life* in the original Greek—"fullness, superabundance, overflowing, limitless." Those adjectives did not describe my life, but I desperately wanted them to. Suddenly I felt the tumultuous excitement of a potential breakthrough to new power.

In rapid-fire order, verses of scripture I had known and memorized were screened on the monitor of my memory. I saw that all of them had something in common. They all revolved around the powerful preposition *in*. The Lord had said that he would be *with* us. But he also promised that he would be *in* us.

> Abide in me, and I in you. . . . Without me ye can do nothing.
>
> JOHN 15:4-5 (KJV)

And suddenly there it was. If life is Christ, the abundant life must be more of him! To be in Christ as believer, disciple, and a loved and forgiven person is one thing. To have Christ in us as motivator, enabler, and transformer of personality is something more. Much more. I knew then what Paul meant when he told the Colossians:

> The mystery hidden for ages and generations but now made manifest to his saints. To them God chose to make known how great are . . . the riches of the glory of this mystery, which is Christ in you, the hope of glory.
>
> COLOSSIANS 1:26-27

Think of it! Our minds, emotions, and wills are

meant to be the post-resurrection home of the immanent, intimate, indwelling Lord!

Closely linked to this discovery was another—the Holy Spirit and the living Christ are one. When Christ promised the gift or comfort of the Holy Spirit (John 14:16-17), he quickly identified himself with the Spirit. "I will come to you," he said. "Yet a little while, and the world will see me no more, but you will see me; because I live, you will live also" (John 14:18-19).

Talk about abundant life! Christ is the revelation of God and the personification of the Holy Spirit. That same Spirit who created all—who dwelt in Christ to save us—that same Spirit is with us now as indwelling Lord. He is with us to give us faith to accept what he did for us as the Messiah, and all he can do through us by forming the fruit of the Spirit—his nature—in us.

> In that day you will know that I am in my Father,
> and you in me, and I in you.
>
> JOHN 14:20

It was 1957. Eight years before, the Lord had created the sense of need, given me the gift of faith, and had become my Savior. Then he waited patiently for me to run out of my own resources in an effort to live the new life in him. All alone with him that summer afternoon at the end of my weary journey of self-propelled discipleship, I invited him to fill me with his Spirit. I have never been the same since.

Vividly I remember my first Sunday back in my pulpit. How could I explain what had happened? I wanted to find a way which would help my people understand and share my discovery. Most of all, I wanted the new

Christians who were in Christ to experience the delight and dynamic of Christ being in them.

It happened. The abundant life became a shared gift of the whole church. We went on together.

Since then the passion and purpose of my life has been to help Christians find the second half of the blessing—life in all its fullness. Recently I was part of a group of leaders from various professions who were asked to identify what they did without using their titles. My answer was direct and simple: "I have the privilege of spending my time helping people discover life without limits."

2

The Other Half

IS IT POSSIBLE we are cut from the same cloth, you and I? Strong-willed people, self-programmed to make it on our own even though we love and believe in Christ? It is difficult to admit our impotence and need, and yet if we are honest the time comes when we acknowledge we are tired of the struggle. We wonder why our faith is so inadequate to help.

I offer you Christ's promise, "I have come that men may have life, and may have it in all its fullness" (NEB)—a two-part blessing.

We cannot have the second without the first. That must be said. But if we have the first without the second, our Christianity will continue to be a grim struggle.

It is not my intention to play down the magnificent first half of the blessing—"I am come that you may have life." The Greek word used here is *zōē*, meaning "essential life." It is more than *bios* or *sōma* (physical life); or *psuchē* (thought and emotional life). Jesus speaks here of the quality of the eternal life he came to give.

He came to take us out of the warp of the power of sin and death. The charter of life he offers is in the kingdom of God, the liberating power is in his death on Calvary, and the defeat of death is in an open tomb. The purpose of Christ's incarnation was to do battle with the enemies of life and free us to live now—and forever. When we believe in Christ, we are ushered into a life over which death has no permanent power. Our sins are forgiven. We are released from self-condemnation. We are free to love ourselves as unreservedly loved by him.

Remember when you first knew the Lord loved you? When you experienced the first half of his blessing? What G. K. Chesterton said, in his *Life of Browning,* about the poet, we can say of our Savior. "He was a kind of cosmic detective who walked into the foulest of thieves' kitchens and accused men publicly of virtue."

Jesus who said of himself, "I am the life," has given us the gift of life. Life beyond time. Forever. We did not deserve it. We could never earn it.

So what is wrong with being satisfied with that kind of blessing? "Sounds adequate to me," you say. And so it is to the majority of Christians.

But something happens as the years go by. We forget that the capacity of faith itself was a gift. We begin to act as if it were by some virtue of our own we decided to become a Christian. The distance between us and Christ widens as we try to serve him in our own strength.

Soon we substitute a personal relationship for the carefully worded creeds and celebrations of the Christian year. We pray and sing our way through Christmas, Good Friday, and Easter. The ho hum of formalized familiarity sets in.

And one by one the old problems return like demons to the empty house. We struggle to be faithful and moral. We try to deal with life's problems. Christ is out there somewhere. We pray our prayers with little feeling of intimacy. The Lord who freed us from self-condemnation and ushered us into a deathless life becomes an awesome Holy Other of a formal I-thou relationship. But we call him in to help when our own management of life breaks down, and then we wonder why he is so slow to respond to our imperious demands.

The problem of the half-blessed Christian is his or her lack of auxiliary power for life's struggles. The half-blessed Christian is befuddled and often immobilized by the perplexity of his or her own human nature. In "My Name Is Legion," Edward Sanford Martin said:

> Within my earthly temple there's a crowd;
> There's one of us that's humble, one that's proud,
> There's one that's broken-hearted for his sins,
> There's one that unrepentant sits and grins;
> There's one that loves his neighbor as himself,
> And one that cares for naught but fame and pelf.
> From much corroding care I should be free
> If I could once determine which is me.

Do you ever feel that way? Defeated over your own nature? Revolted over your thoughts, fantasies, actions, and reactions? Do you wonder how long you dare call yourself a Christian when there is so little of Christ's peace, power, and love in your life?

The apostle Paul's honesty and vulnerability about his own personal tensions is endearing. He shared his struggles. On one occasion he turned a viscerally honest conversation he had with himself into a part of his letter to the church at Rome. It is a letter few modern leaders would dare to write:

> I often find that I have the will to do good, but not the power. That is, I don't accomplish the good I set out to do, and the evil I don't really want to do I find I am always doing. Yet if I do things that I don't really want to do then it is not, I repeat, "I" who do them, but the sin which has made its home within me. When I come up against the Law I want to do good, but in practice I do evil. My conscious mind wholeheartedly endorses the Law, yet I observe an entirely different principle at work in my nature. This is in continual conflict with my conscious attitude, and makes me an unwilling prisoner to the law of sin and death. In my mind I am God's willing servant, but in my own nature I am bound fast, as I say, to the law of sin and death. It is an agonizing situation, and who on earth can set me free from the clutches of my own sinful nature?
>
> ROMANS 7:18-24 (PHILLIPS)

In classical simplicity Paul has described the flip side of the half-blessed life. He has polarized the difference between having religion and having a deep relationship with the indwelling Christ. Charles Kingsley must have arrived at this same dark intersection. "What I want is not to possess a religion," he said, "but to have a religion that shall possess me." And John Oxenham in "Credo":

> Not what, but *Whom,* I do believe,
> That, in my darkest hour of need,
> Hath comfort that no mortal creed
> To mortal man may give.
> Not what, but *Whom!*

It is a very special gift from the Lord when we experience the crisis of the inadequacy of the "what" of religion and want the "whom" of dynamic faith.

A moment ago I interrupted the apostle Paul as he was asking: "Who on earth can set me free from the clutches of my own sinful nature?" He answers his own question:

> I thank God there is a way out through Jesus Christ our Lord. No condemnation now hangs over the head of those who are "in" Jesus Christ. For the new spiritual principle of life "in" Christ lifts me out of the old vicious circle of sin and death.
> ROMANS 7:25—8:2 (PHILLIPS)

Our commitment to Christ is only a beginning. The Lord longs to give us more and more. Remember when he said, "To him who has will more be given, and he will have abundance; but from him who has not, even what he has will be taken away" (Matthew 13:12), RSV). That startling statement is a special assurance to half-blessed Christians. We have the blessing of initial faith. We are now ready to receive in abundance.

The second half of the blessing is the abundance of Christ himself. It is the promise of the fruit of the Spirit. Not what, but whom. Not then but now. Not near but here. Not only Christ with us, but Christ in us. "Christ in you, the hope of glory."

If the first half of our blessing is eternal life, the second half is abundant life. To be in Christ is one thing. To have Christ in us is sublimely more wonderful!

3

That Inner Splendor

PAUL TOLD THE Colossians that the indwelling presence of Christ in the believer—the fruit of the Spirit—was a mystery before Pentecost. Too many Christians live like it still is. Why is it so difficult to talk simply and clearly about what it means to have God dwelling in us?

Let me risk a description of what has been the experience of some of us at least. When we say that Christ pervades all the aspects of our human nature, it does not mean that he effects a takeover of our will. He did not do that before we became his children; he does not do it now. It does mean that when we set our hearts in the direction of what we know to be God's heart in the matter—and begin to model our behavior in that direction—the Spirit within immediately reinforces our finite strength with infinite strength. The synthesis is so smooth, it is sometimes impossible to tell where our strength ends and his begins.

That has always been the signature of the Spirit at work. "The wind blows where it wills, and you hear the sound of it, but you do not know whence it comes or whither it goes; so it is with every one who is born of the Spirit" (John 3:8).

When we say that Christ who is in us possesses our minds, that does not mean he will do our thinking for us without any involvement on our part. Some of us have learned that the hard way. You might say that he exercises a kind of dual control. He scans our conscious and subconscious thought. When we are out of sync with the divine nature, we are made aware of this in almost imperceptible ways and are reminded of the "auxiliary" power his presence provides to make any adjustments.

To have the mind of Christ is to be able to make the same decisions Christ would make under the same circumstances. The interaction with the mind of Christ transforms our thinking about ourselves, others, and life itself. "As he [a person] thinketh in his heart, so is he" (Proverbs 23:7, KJV).

Another translation of the word Paul uses for *mind* is attitude—thought in action. We can have the attitude of Christ for all of life. We can have his perspective on people, problems, and potentials. Life in all its fullness begins with the liberating experience of a renewed mind.

There is more. A great deal more. Jesus promised we would receive power when the Holy Spirit comes upon us. Power to continue the mission he started. And with that power would come special gifts his indwelling presence would teach us to use in each given circumstance.

Look at the liberating legacy of the abundant life Paul described in 1 Corinthians 12. Wisdom. Knowledge. Faith to attempt the impossible. Power to heal. To work miracles. Prophecy. Discernment. And the bonus gift of unfettered praise! All are part of the superabundant equipment for living empowered by the indwelling Christ.

Another aspect of the ministry of the indwelling Spirit is the gift of clarity about what we are to do and be. Nothing debilitates our energies more than indecision. We need more than the advice of others. More than our own seasoned insight or tested experience. Paul found this to be true and learned to defer to the indwelling Spirit in prayer.

> And in the same way—by our faith—the Holy Spirit helps us with our daily problems and in our praying. For we don't even know what we should pray for, nor how to pray as we should; but the Holy Spirit prays for us with such feeling that it cannot be expressed in words. And the Father who knows all hearts knows, of course, what the Spirit is saying as he pleads for us in harmony with God's own will.
> ROMANS 8:26-27 (TLB)

The abundant life is also expressed through the fruit or character of the Spirit—the particular subject of this book. When the living Christ resides in us, he expresses himself through our personalities. Something startling and winsome happens to us ordinary people when the indwelling Christ is given full access to the throne room of our lives.

Paul had a reason for confronting the Galatians with an inventory of what they could be in Christ. They had lost the freedom he had introduced them to when he had helped them know Christ and receive his Spirit. The Galatians were in a state of arrested spiritual development.

If ever a family of believers started out well, they

did. They began their Christian life in the Spirit (Galatians 3:3). The Spirit taught them how to pray (4:6), and how to conduct themselves (5:13-16). Christ had set them free from something many of us know about—the compulsiveness of an inherited religion with its rigidity, rules, and regulations.

But something happened. They were on the brink of going back into the legalism of the ancient law. Life in Christ had given them a freedom to live what they had been taught by Paul, but there were those who were now saying to new believers, "You have to become a Jew first and fulfill all the obligations like we did before you can go on to freedom in Christ." These were the Judaizers, those who said you had to become a Jew before you could become a Christian.

Was there suspense or tension in the Galatian congregation as Paul's letter was read? Indeed! The message was patently clear. Your new life in Christ is not marked by ceremonies, he was saying, but by the celebration of love, joy, peace, patience, kindness, goodness, faithfulness, gentleness, and self-control. The hallmark graces of a new creature in Christ, he went on to say, are not governed by law. His strong implication was that they were not intended to make Christians split personalities either. "If we live by the Spirit," Paul wrote, "let us also walk by the Spirit" (Galatians 5:25).

Have you discovered any Galatian ghettos in the churches of America—where God is seen as an awesome kind of cosmic policeman trying to catch us doing something wrong? Or where the Holy Spirit is seen as a private, separate specter of the Trinity, a mystical power that a person can tap into and receive what other believers do not have. Even the faith of persons who have recognized their sin, accepted God's forgiveness, and have made a commitment of as much as they know of themselves to as much as they know of God can congeal into a set of creeds: ideas to be memorized; a subculture to support; denominational pride to maintain. In this type of situation, the whole dimension of the enabling power of the Spirit is missing. As in Galatia, the problem compounds in dealing with newcomers to the faith.

Also this is painfully illustrated for the Christian parent. The question persists: How do you produce an honest, resolute, consistent, authentic Christian child?

Most of us have faced it in so many inadequate ways. We cajole, punish, barter, manipulate to somehow get children to do what they ought to do. We have told them about what it means to be an ideal Christian, but we have never explained to them what we do with our failures, our vulnerabilities, and our inadequacies when we fail. The whole idea that we always have to be stronger, more adequate, more powerful, more convinced, and more faithful than our children is to tell them a lie and to keep them from experiencing the one power that will enable them to be like Jesus Christ.

The greatest gift you can give a child is to share with the child the very qualities we yearn to develop in him or her and to tell that child that Christian character cannot be earned. It cannot be inherited from Christian parents. Christian character is the result of Christ in us making us like himself. He wants to take up his post-resurrection place in our hearts.

His presence there offers us an antidote to our struggles. Love for our self-condemnation. Joy for our discouraging hours. Peace for our anxieties. Patience for our pressures. Kindness for our hostilities. Goodness for our inconsistencies. Faithfulness for our vacillations. Gentleness for our judgmentalism. Self-control for our turbulent desires for fulfillment.

Another gnawing question demands an answer. Why are so many Christians half-blessed? Why are so many satisfied with the assurance of eternal life, but miss life in all its fullness now? Why did I struggle for eight years trying my best to be a Christian on my own strength? That is what Charles Wesley asked:

> O who can explain
> This struggle for life!
> This travail and pain,
> This trembling and strife!

No one can explain it, but the Lord can change it. He offers us the second half of the blessing. The Holy Spirit—empowered, abundant life. The fruit of the Spirit.

Have you ever asked to be filled with the Spirit? Why not? Fear and caution hold some of us back. We are afraid of losing control. Pride is the culprit with many others who have been Christians and church members for years. We do not want anyone to know how empty we have been.

Others of us, if the truth were known, are not attempting anything grand enough to demand power greater than our own. Pentecostal power is given for a Pentecostal task. But the Lord is patient. You and I, if we have made a commitment to Christ, have the qualifying credits of the first half of the blessing. "To him who has will more be given" (Matthew 13:12). Why not move on?

Tell the Lord that you do not want to be a vague half-believer anymore. Say it! Life in all its fullness can be yours with an anointing of your mind and heart by the Spirit. The superabundance of the indwelling Christ, the second half of the blessing, can happen right now!

4
Extraordinary Love

"OH, HE'S VERY ordinary. And what's more, he's ordinary by choice!"

That was the analysis of a "half-the-stops-out" person. Ordinary by choice! I cannot imagine a more demeaning verdict of a person.

Lincoln said, "The Lord prefers common looking people, that is the reason He makes so many of them." But God has made no ordinary people. We become that by our own choice not to be great people. Each of us is special, unique.

Jesus Christ came to reveal extraordinary living. He called a new breed of humanity to live in him and allow him to live in them. The extraordinary life is receiving and communicating extraordinary love: Christ's love as he lived it; his love in us; and our love motivated by him.

I think it is important to note that the word *fruit* in Paul's code name is not pluralized by him. He does not say: "The fruits of the Spirit *are*. . . . " To do so would seem to pluralize the unity of the image he has chosen to illustrate this inner splendor, this divine life force within us. The word *fruit* is singular for a second reason. It represents the one and only source from which godly character can flow—the spirit of Christ himself.

The fruit of the Spirit is love. . . .

Paul selected a Greek word for "love" that is generally used to express divine love as distinct from human love or friendship. This divine dimension of extraordinary love will affect all loves, but we are called to be containers and transmitters of God's love to the world. The life and message of Christ reveals it; his presence in us elevates us beyond the ordinary to experience and express it. This love, which is a fruit of his indwelling in us, is unmotivated, lived on the millionth mile, and impossible for us on our own. The extraordinary love Jesus requires in the Sermon on the Mount is what he inspires when he comes to make his home in us. The fruit of the Spirit in love is the same quality of love that Jesus taught in the Sermon on the Mount and lived out all through his life. He returned at Pentecost to make such love possible in the extraordinary lovers who came to be known as the Christians.

Do not miss the astonishment of the disciples when they first heard about this divine dimension of love. It was not a love that comes naturally for people we like. It is love that gives us resiliency in our resentment and release from recrimination. The love Jesus taught is more than family affection (*storgē*); far more than the passion of human love (*erōs*); infinitely more than warm friendship (*philia*). Christ's love is unconquerable acceptance and benevolence for people regardless of what they do or who they are.

The Sermon on the Mount confronts us with the essential nature of this love. It is unmotivated. Nothing that the recipient does do or refuses to do stirs its sublime power. Just as God's love for us in Christ was not motivated by our accomplishments or adequacy, so too the fruit of the Spirit in us is a love that is not motivated by the person who needs it. That is exactly what makes it extraordinary. It comes from God. His spirit in us is the only motivation. Matthew 5:38-48 is our charter offering as the secret of love for people we resent and those who have become our enemies. Read it again in preparation for our consideration of the gift of unmotivated love we want to claim in this chapter.

I once talked to a man who was being eaten alive by his resentments. In an hour's conversation, I counted twenty times that he said, directly or indirectly, that he was resentful. He had come to see me about a growing sense of anxiety. The cause became obvious to me. He had turned his resentments in on himself. Because he said he was a Christian, he had forbidden himself ever to get angry. But he was angry—at people, at life in general, and, in a way, at God. The virus of resentment had attacked his soul. And resentment, like revenge, is not sweet. It is poison!

How about you? Do you ever feel put upon, misused, harmed, misunderstood, taken for granted? How do you handle it when people do or say things which hurt or hinder you? Listen to your own words. "I resent that!" "I resent what he does!" "I resent the way you relate to me!"

In this passage from the Sermon on the Mount, Jesus reiterates the *lex talionis* or ordinary love. "You have heard that it was said, 'An eye for an eye and a tooth for a tooth'" (Matthew 5:38). It was based on Exodus

41

21:23-24: "You shall give life for life, eye for eye, tooth for tooth, hand for hand, foot for foot, burn for burn, wound for wound, stripe for stripe." Actually, the Hebrew people had brought sanity into the bizarre methods of retaliation practiced in the ancient world. It had become common for an injured person to wipe out the whole tribe of the person who had harmed or maligned him. The law of Moses went beyond that to an exact quid pro quo. Even that became refined by the later development of the *Baba Kamma* in which the courts decided the payment of money for injury. But here is Jesus with the alarming, astounding challenge that goes way beyond limited retaliation. He calls for no retaliation at all. "Do not resist one who is evil." That means, "Don't get involved in active retaliation against people who do evil toward you." He then makes it very specific in four kinds of insults which cause us to be resentful.

The first deals with insults to our dignity. "If any one strikes you on your right cheek, turn to him the other also." A right-handed person standing in front of another person would have to use the back of his or her hand to strike the blow. According to rabbinic law, to hit a person with the back of the hand was twice as insulting as to hit him or her with the flat of the hand.

The insults we suffer come not so much from the flat of the hand as the flatly stated injury of words spoken to or about us. And Jesus says offer the other cheek. Now we see why we need the unmotivated quality of extraordinary love. What insults linger in your memory? When things people have said drift back to us through the gossip network, we feel anger and resentment. We want to get back at the person, return the volley. We hurt.

We need the fruit of love when forgiveness is required. Only a fresh experience of Christ's forgiveness can enable us to forgive and not return a retributive insult. Or we say, "I'll forgive, but I won't forget!" That is just another way of saying that we will not forgive. Only Christ can help us fulfill Paul's challenge, "Be kind to one another, tenderhearted, forgiving one another, as God in Christ forgave you" (Ephesians 4:32). Forgiveness was so crucial to the Master that it was the only dimension of the Lord's Prayer that he reiterated for emphasis. "If you forgive men their trespasses, your heavenly Father also will forgive you; but if you do not forgive men their trespasses, neither will your Father forgive your trespasses" (Matthew 6:14-15). The parable of the unmerciful servant nails that down tighter than we would like. A king wanted to settle his accounts with debtors. One owed him ten thousand talents. A talent was worth about one thousand dollars. Ten million dollars! What a debt. We are shocked. The debtor could not pay. The king followed the law of the land. The servant and his family were sentenced to slavery. And yet, when the man begged the king for mercy, he forgave the debt. We would expect that servant to be the most magnanimous man alive after that. Instead, immediately he went to find one of his debtors who owed him one hundred denarii—twenty dollars at most. He demanded payment. What a contrast. Twenty dollars in contrast to ten million! When the servant's debtor could not pay, he took him by the throat, throttled him, and threw him into prison. The point of Jesus' story is not what the king's servant did before his forgiveness, but what he did afterward. But news like that travels fast. It got back to the king. The king revoked his previous forgiveness and handed the servant over not just to the prison but to the torturers.

The conclusion of the parable is frightening. We cannot tear it from our Bibles. Jesus said, "So also my heavenly Father will do to every one of you, if you do not forgive your brother from your heart" (Matthew 18:35). That shakes us in our boots! The word *heart* is the key. Only the fruit of love, Christ's love, can give us the power to forgive from our hearts. When our hearts are his home, he does the forgiving through us. Alexander Pope was right: "To err is human, to forgive divine."

Next Jesus focuses on the invasion of a person's rights. "If any one would sue you and take your coat, let him have your cloak as well" (Matthew 5:40). The coat, or tunic as other translations render it, was a *chitōn*, a long inner garment of cotton or linen. Most people had several of these. The cloak was more valuable. It was a great, blanket-like garment worn as outer clothing by day and used as a blanket by night. Ancient Hebrew law protected that possession. "If ever you take your neighbor's garment in pledge, you shall restore it to him before the sun goes down; for that is his only covering, it is his mantle for his body; in what else shall he sleep?" (Exodus 22:26-27).

To sue a man for his tunic was to take him to court for all he had. It is like saying, "I'll sue you right down to the clothes on your back!" or, "I'll get you for all you've got!" When someone does that, Jesus says, offer him your cloak also. Give him your pledge. Tell him that you want to get to the bottom of his grievances and settle the matter. He is calling for freedom from defensiveness. When our security is in him, we can look at accusations honestly. We are liberated to admit where we have failed and be graciously open where we have not. What a wonderful way to live!

The fruit of love is communicated in a desire to see things as they are. Fortified by the power of such love, we can say to people who accuse us, "Listen, you feel you have a right to what I have because of what you think I've done to you. I want to hear you out, and I promise to seek your forgiveness if after the whole matter is exposed, I have acted wrongly." Or we can say, "You have a grievance against me. I give you my pledge that I want to know what you perceive I've done and settle the matter." And in other words, "If I've hurt you, I want to know how. You have a right to your feelings. I want to know what I might have done." No ordinary love, that!

I know personally and have great admiration for the founders of the Christian Legal Society which seeks to help Christians in the negotiation of conflicts which otherwise could end up in long and costly court battles. My esteemed friend Robert Toms, one of the nation's top attorneys, is one of the founders. Along with others, he has fleshed out Jesus' admonition, "Make friends quickly with your accuser, while you are going with him to court, lest your accuser hand you over to the judge" (Matthew 5:25). These Christian lawyers help people to express the essence of extraordinary love in conflicts. People are encouraged to admit that there are two sides to every issue, and are helped to enter into prayerful negotiation to transform lose-lose situations into win-win resolutions. The most formidable challenge is always to set people free of defensiveness.

Christ in us can free us of that truncated vision. He gives us double vision to look at ourselves and the other person. Resentment over the invasion of our rights is cured by a growing sense of righteousness with the Lord.

But what about our pride? Jesus goes on to confront inflictions to our pride. He does that with an example familiar to all his listeners in saying that if anyone forces you to go one mile, you should go with him two miles. In Jesus' time, a Roman soldier could lay his sword on the shoulder of any Jew and make him carry a load like a beast of burden. It was an excruciating insult. Roman roads were marked off in one-mile sections. It was as if Jesus was saying, "If a Roman compels you to go a mile, keep the load on your back and astound him by going the second mile." The Greek word *aggareuein* (compel), from the word *aggareus*, actually came from the Persian postal service word meaning "courier." The Persian couriers could impress people or their property into their service at will. Eventually the word came to mean the power of an occupying army to conscript a conquered people into the most menial tasks.

When we combine this statement by Jesus with his admonitions about forgiveness to Peter, we realize that he meant not only the second mile, but the millionth mile of living. The reluctant disciple wanted to set limits on forgiveness. "As many as seven times?" The Master's immediate reply was a Hebraism which meant without limits, "I do not say to you seven times, but seventy times seven" (Matthew 18:22). The same is true when our pride is injured by what people do to us.

We feel resentment when people ask us to do something which is beneath us because we are over qualified, or when they neglect to ask us to do something for which we are eminently qualified. Our feelings are out of sorts too much of the time. The sights and oversights rankle us. We stew in our own emotional juices, all because our security is misplaced. There is no limit to the good we can do when we do not care who gets the glory and recognition. But that takes more than ordinary love.

The fourth thing Jesus confronts is intrusions on our

46

privacy. The three most important human commodities we have are time, experience, and money. We all feel resentment when people demand our time when it is not convenient or when we are under pressure. They impose as if they were the only people alive and all we have to do is to be with them. Also we resent people who refuse to do their own homework and leech on our learning and experience hammered out in years of hard work. We all feel mixed reactions when we are assailed by poachers, beggars, and friends who want money we have worked hard to earn. Once I was accosted by a man on the street who asked me for a dollar—not for a cup of coffee, but for a beer! Another person on the street said what we all feel at times, "I don't know why these people don't work for a living like the rest of us." But most disturbing to us are our friends and relatives who never become independent and are constantly on our doorstep wanting us to support their irresponsibility.

Then we hear Jesus call for extraordinary giving as an expression of love. "Give to him who begs from you, and do not refuse him who would borrow from you" (Matthew 5:42). The more I ponder that, the more dependent I am on the Lord to live it. From within he reminds me that all that I have and am is his gift. Without him I could not breathe a breath, think a thought, write a sentence, preach a message, earn a dime, or develop my life. All that I have is from him to be given away lavishly. We often hear the old shibboleth, "You can't take it with you." Wrong! We will take our souls with us into eternity. What we have done with the outer resources will dramatically affect the inner person that death cannot destroy. The parable of the rich man and Lazarus drives that frightening point closer to home than we like.

Most people do not need the material things we can give or lend, but rather they need our love. That is the deeper implication of Jesus' admonition. It is easy to give a handout and hope we will never see the person again. Instead of a dollar for a beer for the man on the street, it took three dollars for a meal and hours of my time and the members of Alcoholics Anonymous in my church to set the man free of his compulsive alcoholism by helping him to experience Christ's love and forgiveness. People who are habitually in need of money really need help to get on their feet, not evasively stay off them. They require prolonged times of counseling and an introduction to the Savior. That means not just our time, but ourselves. I could not take the pressures of human need in Los Angeles and the burdens of people who come to town seeking help as a result of our national television ministry, if it were not for the team of extraordinary lovers in the laity of my church who have discovered that to be in Christ is to be in ministry. No pastor can see all the people who need him. He was never meant to. The ministry of compassion is given to all the congregation.

To be free to give ourselves away is the fruit of Christ the vine. When we are branches attached to the unlimited source of love, we are never alone or without an adequate flow of healing grace for others.

There is a difference between "getting even" and "even getting." One is the way of resentment; the other the way of release. Getting even is normal life stretched to the breaking point and severed. Even getting is proportionate inflow and outgo. We are never asked to give more than we have received. We are channels, not holding tanks, of love. If we get to a place where the resources have run out, we need to check our connection to the vine. No root, no fruit!

Jesus goes on in the Sermon on the Mount to give us the specific steps of communicating extraordinary love. He does it in contrast to current teaching of the time: "You shall love your neighbor and hate your enemy." His startling challenge was, "Love your enemies, bless those who curse you, do good to those who hate you, and pray for those who spitefully use you and persecute you" (Matthew 5:44, NKJB-NT). The key to expressing that kind of love is in the experience of the family characteristic of God's character shared with His children: "That you may be sons of your Father who is in heaven" (Matthew 5:45, NKJB-NT). Jesus tells us that we can be like God in the communication of his love. I would like to suggest a reordering of the active verbs *love, bless, do good,* and *pray* in a progression that works for me. It is consistent with the Lord's total message and gives us some specific steps to take in being extraordinary lovers.

Start with prayer. Talk to the Lord about the person you find it difficult to love. Ask the Lord to show you the deeper reason. In conversation, allow God to give you his perspective on the person and his or her needs you may not have known. In the quiet, picture the person as loved by God and filled with his Spirit. Claim that it will be so!

Next, ask for the gift of love for that person. Tell the Lord that you cannot love him or her by yourself. Ask for a special infilling of giving and forgiving love that only the Lord can give.

Now, put that into words to the person. To bless is to belong and to be beloved. We are beloved by God to bless others. Most people need to hear in words what the Lord has helped us to feel. Answer this question: What could I say that would help that person to know I am for him or her, that nothing can change my attitude?

People desperately need affirmation and encouragement.

Lastly, as a companion to words of love, "do good" to the person. What is the loving act that will make our words believable? The Lord will help us discern what that is. Love is what we do along with what we say.

Whenever I follow these simple, decisive steps, the fruit of love changes me and then the relationship. And I discover what Jesus meant when he concluded this section of the Sermon on the Mount. "Therefore you shall be perfect, just as your Father in heaven is perfect" (Matthew 5:48, NKJB-NT). The word for "perfect" in Greek is *teleioi* from *telos* meaning purpose, end, goal. The purpose of our lives is to be loved and to love. Living is for loving.

No one can read or digest Jesus' explanation of extraordinary love without exclaiming, "That's impossible!" The response is exactly what Jesus expected and wanted. If we could do it by ourselves, we would not need the precious fruit of his love. That leaves us with a perturbing question, "What are we attempting in loving others that we could never pull off without the indwelling power of the Lord's love?" We were never meant to be ordinary. Unmotivated love is the authentic hallmark of a Spirit-filled Christian.

5

I've Got the Joy.
Let's Get to Work!

"I'VE GOT THE joy. Let's get to work!" That was the post-party challenge my wife gave the family when all the friends had left and the kitchen sink was filled with dirty pans.

Not a bad motto for life! What she meant was that she had the Joy detergent and wanted some help cleaning up the mess. It is fascinating to count the number of products on the supermarket shelves named for disappearing virtues of life today. Joy is certainly one of them. But there is no facsimile for real joy.

Joy is the second character trait awaiting development in us listed under Paul's code name *fruit*.

The fruit of the Spirit is joy.

Joy is not gush or ho-ho jolliness. It is more than happiness. It is impervious to difficult situations and impossible people. Joy is an outward expression of grace, God's unmotivated love. The Greek word for "grace" is *charis* and the word for "joy" is *chara*. They both come from the same root.

I want to tackle a disturbing question. Why are there so many dogged, joyless, do-it-yourself Christians? We see them everywhere. Some experience sporadic, fleeting moments of joy, but they are not lasting or consistent. Allow me to suggest a possible answer that has been growing to conviction-sized proportions in my mind.

Joy is the result of being loved by God. When his undeserved grace and forgiveness penetrates through the thick layers of self-doubt and self-negation, we begin to feel the surge of joy. Self-esteem and joy go together. We can joyously exclaim, "I'm glad I'm me!" That is not easy for most Christians. We find it difficult to let God love us and change our demeaning self-image. It takes a constant reminder of how much God loves us. The Cross alone can balance off the weighted scales loaded with self-condemnation.

But why is it that Christians who have heard about the grace of God repeatedly still miss the joy? There are several reasons; each presses us deeper into an understanding of true joy.

The first is that there can be no joy without Christ living in us. His promises about joy are all connected to realizing a profound intimacy with him. Like love, joy flows from the vine into the branch. When we abide in him and he in us, we know joy. In John 15, after Jesus had taken great care to explain his "I Am" assertion that he was the true vine from whom our spiritual vitality flows, he said, "These things I have spoken to you, that my joy may be in you, and that your joy may be full." R. Leonard Small's now classic statement summarizes the promise. "Joy is the standard that flies on the battlements of the heart when the King is in residence." Jesus Christ himself is our joy!

The second salient reason many people miss the joy is that Jesus promised joy in the midst of difficulties. In John 16 he told us that we would know sorrow and disappointment but that it would be a prelude to experiencing new joy. He used the image of a woman in childbirth. The birth process is not easy. Like any of the hopes and dreams which grow in us, it is often painful. But because of the joy of the birth, the anguish is soon forgotten.

> So you have sorrow now, but I will see you again and your hearts will rejoice, and no one will take your joy from you. . . . Truly, truly, I say to you, if you ask anything of the Father, he will give it to you in my name. Hitherto you have asked nothing in my name; ask, and you will receive, that your joy may be full.
>
> JOHN 16:22-24

The conclusion of Jesus' message there in the upper room gives the secret source of joy. His honest statement about reality is coupled with the assurance of his victory over evil and death. He faced the cross with this assurance: "Yet I am not alone, for the Father is with me" (v. 32). Then he gave the disciples the liberating legacy for joy. "I have said this to you, that in me you may have peace. In the world you have tribulation; but be of good cheer, I have overcome the world" (v. 33).

Joy is not something we know only when everything is smooth and easy. It is not spiritual ecstasy when all the problems are solved. Rather, joy is the special fruit of the indwelling Christ in the actual experience of problems. The reason so many Christians miss the joy is that they keep waiting for a time when life's complications will be resolved. We think of joy as compensation for working things out for the Lord. Instead, true joy is his companionship during the battle, not only after the battle. Many of us feel we have no right to feel joyous as long as we are not perfect, still have areas in which we need to grow, and continue to face unresolved tensions. Joy is for the journey, not just for the reflective moments after the journey.

The essential difference between happiness and joy is that happiness is usually circumstantial and situational. The root of the meaning of *happiness* is *hap,* meaning "chance"; the root of joy is changeless love.

When the King is in residence we are able to fight life's battles with joy. We become "overcomers." Troublesome people and frustrating situations, pressures and challenges, disappointments and grief, heartache and sorrow will all be infused with joy, because we know that the Lord will use them all for our growth and his glory.

A journalist caught the meaning of joy in Pope John Paul II. He said Pope John Paul seemed to convey always an almost tangible sense of strength and extraordinary low-burning joy, joy in adversities endured . . . in being a Christian and in being human.

Many of us deny our humanity in our search for joy. Life is run on two tracks, one of bold beliefs and the other of life's difficulties. A Spirit-filled Christian can dare to bring the two together. We can be honest with ourselves and the Lord about what we are going through and feeling. Surrender is the key. When we turn our real world over to our Lord and know that he will work everything together for good, the fruit of joy is expressed in our character and countenance.

When we block the Lord out of our real needs, thinking we should be responsible to work those out ourselves, we checkmate him from reaching us where we need him most desperately. That has been difficult for me to learn. There is still that lingering misconception that if I were more faithful and obedient, there would be no pressing needs in my life.

Once I went through a confrontation with a person I love very much. He had some things to say that hurt deeply. Afterwards, I had a bad case of the "if only's." Do you ever get them? As long as I dealt with my feelings defensively, there was no joy. Then I was brought to my knees in my heart again. "Lord, what can I learn from this? What are you trying to tell me? I hurt, Lord, and need you very much!" Joy flooded my heart. The situation was not resolved completely, but joy returned. I knew that the One who gives each day would show the way. There were things I needed to do and say to correct the problem, but I was able to do them with joy.

The same thing has happened to me all through my life and ministry. Joy was given me as a fruit of the Spirit years ago. The harvesting and sowing of the gift have usually come in the midst of stretching challenges and soul-sized opportunities.

I write this with you in mind. Perhaps you are going through something right now that is painful and excruciating. Most of us are. There will always be problems. That is life. But there will also be more than adequate strength. That is joy. Do not wait until the crisis is over to allow yourself the delicious fruit of joy. True joy is but a prayer of surrender away. Get in touch with where you are hurting and hoping. That will be the focus of a new joy. In a decade of diminishing energy resources, you should know that you can count on the Lord's joy to fuel and reinforce your human spirit in all possible (and impossible!) situations. Praise God for crises. They are fresh opportunities to experience joy.

In preparation for writing this chapter, I did a comprehensive review of the word *joy* in scripture. It is almost always experienced in the context of some difficulty or in reflection on what the Lord had made of the raw material of discouragement. What the Lord will do, is doing, and has done is our joy.

The prayer of Habakkuk has become one of my favorites. It reminds us that the fruit of joy is produced when other harvests are barren.

> Though the fig tree do not blossom,
>   nor fruit be on the vines,
> the produce of the olive fail
>   and the fields yield no food,
> the flock be cut off from the fold
>   and there be no herd in the stalls,
> yet I will rejoice in the Lord,
>   I will joy in the God of my salvation.
> God, the Lord, is my strength;
>   he makes my feet like hinds' feet,
>   he makes me tread upon my high places.
>   HABAKKUK 3:17-19

Note the way the word *joy* is used as part of the future verb form of the Hebrew. Not, "I will have joy," but, "I will joy"! The same is true with the Holy Spirit's fruit. A noun becomes a verb for daily living. Not a bad commitment for all of life. "I will joy—regardless."

Another verse which gives us the distilled meaning of joy is Acts 13:52, "And the disciples were filled with joy and the Holy Spirit." They had every reason not to be. They had just been through a hard time of rejection and persecution in Antioch of Pisidia. Note what happened just before the disciples experienced the fresh flush of joy in the Holy Spirit. "The Jews incited the devout women of high standing and the leading men of the city, and stirred up persecution against Paul and Barnabas, and drove them out of their district. But they shook off the dust from their feet against them, and went to Iconium" (*vv.* 50-51).

I like that. Joy was not dependent on human success, the approval of people, or having everything go right. The disciples could press on to the next challenge. The Holy Spirit gave them joy for the next steps of the strategy. Paul is always very clear about the source of joy. It is "inspired by the Holy Spirit" (1 Thessalonians 1:6).

But there is a further reason some contemporary Christians miss the joy. True joy is part of God's nature which he wants to share with his children. It is a family characteristic. What gives God joy is the source of our joy. In fact, there is no lasting joy until we are partners with God in what he is doing in the world. According to the parabolic teaching of Jesus, God experiences joy whenever we join him in concern for the lonely and the lost. The old gospel song says, "If you want joy, real joy, let Jesus come into your heart." That is fine as far as it goes. We should also sing, "If you want to keep joy, real joy, let Jesus flow out of your heart to others."

In the parables of the lost son, the sheep, and the coin, Jesus tells us that God and the whole company of heaven have sublime joy when the lost are found. The elder brother missed sharing that joy. The shepherd who left the ninety-nine sheep in search of the one lost sheep shared the heart of God when he recovered the wandering sheep. And the woman who would not give up until

57

she had found the lost coin tasted the joy of heaven when she found the coin. The "lost and found" department of heaven is always open.

God's joy is the result of love received. He knows no greater joy than when we let him love us. And our joy, as sons and daughters of our heavenly Father, is a by-product of allowing him to love others through us. A personal note: The only greater joy for me than becoming a Christian has been helping other people live forever by introducing them to Christ and salvation. Joy breaks forth in inner splendor when I have been given the privilege of leading another person to the Lord and the great adventure of life in the Lord. Joy becomes a lasting fruit when I am free to love and care, give and forgive, listen to and hope for people.

Whenever Christians tell me they have lost the joy they once had, my first question is, "When was the last time you helped someone meet Christ?" How would you answer that? Who is alive in Christ because of you?

The more I study the parable of the talents in Matthew 25:14-30, the more convinced I become that Jesus had the reproduction of our faith in others in mind. He taught the parable at the end of his ministry. He knew that he was going away, the cross was ahead, and he would be back.

The parable of the talents was based on a custom of the time. Local provincial leaders deployed by the Roman Empire were often called back to Rome. While they were gone, they entrusted their properties and investments to subordinates. Jesus built on the familiar to teach an unfamiliar, and very surprising, truth. We will get the full impact if we identify the "man" going away on a journey with the Lord himself, and the servants with the disciples and with us.

You know the story. One was given one talent, another two, and the other five. Remember, a talent was worth about a thousand dollars. Whether $1,000, $2,000 or $5,000, each was given a great sum to invest. Both the two- and five-talent servants doubled their investment. The one-talent servant was afraid of losing what he had and buried his talent in the ground.

Inevitably, the time of accounting came. Note that the two- and five-talent servants received accolades for their multiplication of their investment and were invited to a very special privilege—the *joy* of the master. The one-talent servant said, "I was afraid, and I went and hid your talent in the ground." The punishment for that was severe. "So take the talent from him," the master said, "and give it to him who has the ten talents. For to every one who has will more be given, and he will have abundance; but from him who has not, even what he has will be taken away. And cast the worthless servant into the outer darkness; there men will weep and gnash their teeth" (Matthew 25:25, 28-30).

The key to understanding the parable is in what Jesus meant by the talent. What is the one thing he promised to entrust to us? The abundant life. And he wants to know what we have done with it. For our teaching about joy, the point is very clear. Those who multiply the gift of new life in him enter into his joy. There is one kind of joy we receive in companionship with the Lord in prayer. There is an even greater joy which comes to us in adventuring with him in involvement with people. To "enter into the joy of the Master" (with a capital M), is to share with others what he means to us. Whatever word you attach to it—soul winning, sharing the faith, evangelism—matters little if the passion of our lives is bringing people to the Lord. We cannot experience deeper joy, or keep it, until we share the love we have received.

Some of us are too busy for that. We refuse to be interrupted by people who are put on our agendas by the Lord. Many of us do not want a life where plans are apt to be canceled for situations of unscheduled human need. There is little place or time for sudden, unrepeatable opportunities to incarnate an act of divine love. We get hung up on what we perceive as our own spiritual maturity, a petulant perfectionism over theological details or do's and don'ts which have little to do with Christ's purpose for us. Many have never discovered that an act of extending God's love or telling another what Christ can do with a life surrendered to him explodes into joy!

There are needy candidates for Christ's love all around us. Love-starved people are everywhere. Unblessed children of loveless marriages. Distraught parents. People locked into the syndrome of sameness. Friends who are anxious and worried. Associates who are missing the reason they were born. Neighbors tied like Gulliver to the accumulation of things, and acquaintances who are more ready to talk about their heartaches than we are to listen. Some of those people will not live forever because we hid the talent of our abundant life in the ground.

Have I written myself into a contradiction? How can the fruit of the Spirit of joy be freely given and yet depend so much on our response? All I have tried to say is that which we will not use, we lose. Joy is ours as a result of grace. But it is for the realities of life. And it lasts as it is given away.

We have come full circle. "I've got the joy. Now let's get to work!" Robert Louis Stevenson was right: "To miss the joy is to miss all."

6
Peace in Life's Pressures

I AM GOING to ask you some very personal questions. Audacious? Maybe. But if you and I could sit down and talk together over a cup of coffee, these are the questions I would like to ask you—and I would like to have you ask me.

What is it that robs you of peace?

Who is it in your life who has the capacity to hassle you to the place that you lose your inner calm—that sense of unity and peace?

What is it in your life that makes you impatient and stretches your innermost to the place of breaking?

Who is it who can rankle you to the place that you lose your countenance and blast that person for what he or she is or has done?

We all have a breaking point, a place where life gets to us, when it is impossible to feel peace or express patience. It is here that the fallacy hits us once again. We have been taught all our lives that peace was something we could condition by thinking the right thoughts.

There is nothing wrong with good mental hygiene, but the peace that will see us through the deep turbulence of our times is not programmed mind control. Such peace cannot be induced by drugs or patched into the fabric of our tissues like an electrode.

Peace is the pearl we would give fortunes for. "Peace," Matthew Henry said, "is such a precious jewel that I would give anything for it but truth."

The fruit of the Spirit is peace.

Our mental institutions are filled with people longing for peace. Walk along any street in any city in America. We can all see the expressions on the faces of people which indicate that in their hearts there is a lack of peace.

Is it any wonder the word was so often on the lips of our Lord? He greeted his disciples with the single word, "Peace!" The early church was characterized by the greeting, "The peace of the Lord Jesus be with you!" A part of the historic eucharist has been: *"Pax tibiti"*— "Peace to you!"

In Hebrew the word for "peace" is *shalom*. In Greek it is *eirēnē*. In Latin it is *pax*. What is this peace?

Peace is more than a state of freedom from hostility, more than harmony or a temporary truce in personal relationships. We need to plumb deeply into the nature of the peace our Lord had in mind when he said:

> Peace I leave with you; my peace I give to you; not
> as the world gives do I give to you.
>
> JOHN 14:27

He gives it to us by virtue of his indwelling presence, the presence Paul spoke of as fruit to imply a process of growth or degrees of development depending on our cooperation. The fruit of peace becomes resplendent in us when our acceptance of God's forgiveness is complete in every level of our being.

There are memories that lurk within us and rob us of peace, memories that rub the conscience raw. When we are quiet, a familiar piece of music or a face we have not seen for a long time floods back into our mind and heart, bringing with it the realization of unresolved failure, sin, or rebellion. And our peace is gone.

Our peace is also shattered when we refuse to be the agent of forgiveness in the lives of other persons. Is there anyone you need to forgive, anyone who has failed you at some point in your life—in your family, the church, or in our society? Very often we carry the burden of restitution and reconciliation so that we actually live as though Christ had not made a once, never-to-be-repeated, substitutionary reconciliation for the sin of the world in his body on the cross.

> In him all the fulness of God was pleased to dwell,
> and through him to reconcile to himself all things,
> whether on earth or in heaven, making peace by the
> blood of his cross.
> COLOSSIANS 1:19-20

We either accept or try to reproduce that magnificent atonement. And very often we fail to forgive all. We take the burden of some failure in another person's life and carry it inside of ourselves. We do it at the cost of trying to reproduce what was done at Calvary on our behalf. "A great many people are trying to make peace," D. L. Moody said, "but that has already been done. God has not left it for us to do; all we have to do is to enter into it."

That came as a result of settling our priorities. Second place is the only place Christ will not take. He was rather severe about the nature of the peace he would offer when he said, "Do not think that I have come to bring peace on earth; I have not come to bring peace, but a sword" (Matthew 10:34). Suddenly our minds are awake to discover the kind of severing he meant.

> He who loves father or mother more than me is not worthy of me; and he who loves son or daughter more than me is not worthy of me. . . . He who finds his life will lose it, and he who loses his life for my sake will find it.
>
> MATTHEW 10:37,39

A lack of peace is a warning signal, a jarring alarm inside us telling us that someone or something has taken Christ's place as Lord of our hearts. Who is it? What is it? Where is it for you?

We all long to be quiet inside, to have an inner unity and oneness. The loss of this peace is the price we pay for a secondary loyalty. Jesus Christ said we cannot possibly serve two masters. Authentic love of one results in hatred for the other. Anytime you feel the terrible disease and dis-quiet it is time to begin to ask, "Who's first in my life? Am I seeking first God's kingdom, his absolute reign and rule in all of life's relationships and responsibilities?"

Are you at peace right now? Is there within you that quiet, that healing distillation that only the Lord can give? The meaning of the word *peace* in both Hebrew and Greek is the knitting together, the unification of what has been broken and unraveled and disrupted. It means wholeness. In fact it is almost a synonym for the meaning of *salvation,* which means oneness and wholeness and unification.

Do I have peace? It is only fair that you should ask me that question, too. I find that though I spend my life studying the scriptures, leading a church, caring for people, and getting more than my share of love and affirmation from these relationships, there are times when I feel an absence of peace. Sometimes—for a moment, day, or a week—I take my eyes off Jesus Christ and put them on some cause or some purpose or something that I willfully want to do. Then when I begin to feel what I have come to call "jangledness" inside, I have to be still and go back to prayer and say, "Lord, what is it that has taken priority over you?"

Do you remember that marvelously clean and uncluttered sentence written by the prophet Isaiah on this very subject? "Thou wilt keep him in perfect peace, whose mind is stayed on thee" (Isaiah 26:3, KJV). That is the answer.

Peace is the companion of knowing and doing the will of God. We cannot be at peace if we have been given marching orders in a particular relationship or sector of our lives and refuse to follow them. Once we say, "Lord, what do *you* want me to do? What do *you* want me to say? How do *you* want me to act?" and consciously refuse to follow the clear distinctive he gives, we will not know peace. Faithful obedience—that is the environment that develops the fruit of peace.

Paul used an athletic term to help the Colossian Christians understand how the peace factor enables us to know what is creative for us and what could be debilitating. He advised, "Let the peace of Christ rule in your hearts" (3:15). The Greek word for "rule" is *umpire.* The indwelling Christ will call the plays—safe or out.

The apostle also spoke of peace as a protector. Listen to this:

> Have no anxiety about anything, but in everything by prayer and supplication with thanksgiving let your requests be made known to God. And the peace of God, which passes all understanding, will keep your hearts and your minds in Christ Jesus.
>
> PHILIPPIANS 4:6-7

The word for "keep" in the phrase "keep your hearts" means to look forward, to watch out for, to stand as a sentinel. Christ's spirit is within us actively surveying the terrain ahead, looking, guarding, monitoring, flashing a warning, breaking the ground ahead of us, navigating us safely through the hidden entanglements and mine-infested debris in the path ahead. He shows us the clear path. When we trust him, there is peace.

It is one thing to have peace, to savor peace, to be managed and protected by this divine implant of the Spirit. But there is one thing more: You can be God's agent in making peace for others. "Blessed are the peacemakers," Jesus said, "for they shall be called sons of God" (Matthew 5:9). The dividends from such an investment of yourself have no equal. To be a peacemaker means to be actively involved with God in the task of reconciling people to himself.

The fruit of peace bears fruit. The fruit of one Christian is another. We are to be reproductive. Our Christian life is not complete until we become active, contagious communicators of Christ's love to others. Each of us was introduced to the Savior by someone who cared enough to become involved in listening and loving. I would not be writing this book if it had not been that two college friends took time to earn the right to show me that my emptiness was a longing for purpose and power which only Christ could give. I saw the peace of Christ in them and wanted what they had. Who is alive in Christ because of you? Who in your life most needs an introduction to Peace himself? Your concern for them is a call to tell them what he has done for you and then, when he or she has been prepared by the Spirit, to be the winsome introducer.

We cannot make peace by ourselves. It is Spirit-grown. But each of us can be God's agent in "making" it with others. That means initiative involvement, being the first to ask for or express forgiveness and restitution.

Each of us can also be God's special agent in reconciling people to each other, as an unassuming, "unofficial" peace presence in the tensions that explode around us. We are to listen to both sides without taking sides. We can go to people who are separated in conflict and misunderstanding. Our task is to open the channels of understanding and empathy. Often it is necessary to help people pray for forgiveness and the power to be forgiving. We will feel the pulse of the heart of God when he yearned over Israel. "They have healed the wound of my people lightly, saying, 'Peace, peace,' when there is no peace" (Jeremiah 8:11). Whenever we get in touch with the anguish in people or identify our own struggles, we realize how much we need the peace of God and how much we need to become peacemakers. The Spirit's peace in us can add a sacramental touch to shared joys and sorrows.

Peace flows into us when we allow it to flow out of us in active peacemaking. A child shares the character and purpose of his or her father. We are truly sons and daughters of God when we are engaged in active peace-making. Today is the time for initiating peace between people and us and between them and others. Anything which keeps people apart is our concern and responsibility as peacemakers. If we want Christ's peace in our hearts, we must be engaged in combating negative criticism, gossip, and innuendos which destroy relationships. Our constant concern will be to help people forgive, accept, and understand one another. Think of what life could be if our sole purpose were to bring reconciliation among our family and friends! Here is a daily motto. Put it on your desk, on the wall of your kitchen, or beside your bed to read when you start each day.

> God was in Christ reconciling the world to himself, not counting their trespasses against them, and entrusting to us the message of reconciliation. So we are ambassadors for Christ, God making his appeal through us.
>
> 2 CORINTHIANS 5:19-20

Finally, peace is the result of the indwelling of the living Christ. Peace is not only a gift of Christ, it is Christ himself living his life in us through the Holy Spirit, his presence in our hearts and minds. It is abiding in Christ and allowing him to abide in us.

Our Lord gives us the gift of capacity to picture what we would be like if his peace dwelt in our hearts. Focus the image of yourself as a peace-possessed person. Now picture your people around you at peace with Christ's love and forgiveness flowing among all your loved ones and friends.

Prayer for peace comes from a lively, Christ-inspired imagination. Once we have the picture, we can ask Christ to give us his legacy of peace. He is more ready to give than we are to ask. Praying for peace begins with him. He motivates us to ask for what he has prepared for us through a manger, a cross, an empty tomb, and a present power. Now we can say and mean, "Peace be with you! May the peace of the living Christ live in your hearts." The fruit of the Spirit is peace.

7
He's Got All the Time in the World

IN ORDER FOR us to model his kind of love in the world, God knew we would need patience—the power to suffer long. It would be naive indeed to think that loving persons with God's love would insure that all of our relationships with them would be congenial.

The fruit of the Spirit is patience.

I was out of town, and I needed a suit cleaned and pressed in a hurry. I found one of those, "fresh as a flower in just one hour," quick cleaning establishments. The sign on the door said, "We cater to impatient people in a hurry." Feeling that I qualified on both counts, I presented my crumpled, well-traveled suit to the owner. He took my name and with an unpleasant attitude demanded, "When do you want it? Yesterday, I suppose!" My first inclination was to grab my suit back and tell him that he could keep his cleaning fluids and the juices of his unpleasantness to himself. My pride got the best of me when I thought of speaking in that wrinkled suit. I pointed to the sign with all the one-hour, for-people-in-a-hurry promises. "Yeah, that's right," he said tempering his tone a bit. "It's been a hard day. I guess I'm 'impatient people'!" We both laughed, the tension was relaxed, and he cleaned and pressed my suit.

As I walked back to my hotel, I reflected on the living parable I had just experienced. The very thing the shop wanted to be known for was the one thing the proprietor was tiring of producing. He wanted to serve impatient people and yet his impatience bristled when asked to do what the sign promised. Then it hit me: I would like to be known as a patient person. I preach about it, try to help others discover it, and yet I find impatience a difficult problem to conquer. I had never met the cleaning man before, and yet his diagnosis was on target: I do like to have everything yesterday!

How about you? Ever troubled with impatience? Do difficult people ever test your patience? Does what they do or fail to do get to you? Are you ever upset when people you love fail to capture your vision for them? Ever get exasperated when people do not meet your expectations of what you want them to accomplish on your time schedule? And more profoundly, knowing people's potential and what the Lord can do with the life given over to his control, do you become impatient with their slow response or imperviousness?

And what about the problems in our society and the world? Does reading the newspaper fill you with indignation bordering on rage? With all our scientific advancement and technological skill, we have not come very far in human progress. Or, what about the slowness of governmental machinery? Does your blood boil over our ineptness and inefficiency in grasping and solving problems? And to top it off, there is the computerized impersonalization of modern business. Have you tried to straighten out a bill you have overpaid or underpaid? And behind it all are people whose goofs and oversights gum up the highly polished machinery. People like you and me!

The greatest source of our impatience is ourselves. Have you been astounded as I have by the little progress you have made in some areas? In your personal life and attitudes? Your relationships? Your work and professional advancement? Most of us could qualify for the sign on the quick cleaning shop. We are impatient and in a hurry. But where are we going so fast?

If we were to get where we are going, where would we be? If we acquired all that we want, what would we have? When it is all over, what is the one-word epitaph they could put on our gravestone? Patient? Not I, nor most of us.

But let's not be too severe on ourselves. Go deeper. Our real problem is finding the balance between a divinely inspired discontent and just accepting ourselves and things as they are. Praise God for the reformers, inventors, and visionaries of history, who did not accept the lie that what is must always be. The people who have helped history turn its crucial corners were people who have had a dream and dared to stick with it. They were patient and impatient all at the same time. Endurance marked their character. They persisted with the vision until it came of age.

Perhaps our problem with impatience is that we misunderstand patience. It is not acquiescence, or perpetual placidity, or feckless lack of fiber. Patience must be rooted in an overarching confidence that there is Someone in control of this universe, our world, and our life. We need to know that things do work together for good for those who love God. A patient person knows the shortness of time and the length of eternity. Patience is really faith in action. No wonder it is called an aspect of the fruit of the Spirit. It is one of the matchless characteristics of Christ himself. If we would learn patience, he alone can teach us. There are many facsimiles of the virtue, but authentic patience comes as a result of deep personal relationship with Christ.

He has given us the secret of this fruit of his indwelling presence.

> Come to me, all who labor and are heavy laden, and I will give you rest. Take my yoke upon you, and learn from me; for I am gentle and lowly in heart, and you will find rest for your souls. For my yoke is easy, and my burden is light.
>
> MATTHEW 11:28-30

The Lord's invitation and promise gives us four salient aspects of how to learn to be patient in his style and by his power.

First of all, Jesus knows about our frustrations and the resulting anger over things, people, and ourselves. To labor and still be heavy laden is to feel trapped by life and by its constricting circumstances. The Lord felt deeply the pain of the economic, political, and religious yokes under which people lived. The future offered little relief. Many of the people were poor. The heel of Rome pressed tightly on their necks with taxes and restrictions of a captured people in occupied land. But the greatest concern to the Master was the endless labor to do the works of the law with faithfulness and the burdens which the scribes imposed with rules and regulations. He

74

appealed to people who had tried to please God by ful-
filling the letter of the law and failed. His invitation has
echoed down through the centuries to people who are
burdened by life and their own inability to change themselves or the life around them.

Jesus Christ invites the impatient to come to him,
those who have tried to be faithful and creative and have
not been able to pull it off. Only a person who has
values, standards, and a vision of what life can be is
impatient with himself, other people, or circumstances.
In substance, he says to us, "Come to me, I understand
the disappointment and frustration you feel.; I know
your integrity and the heartache you experience when
you miss the mark. I want to give you a gift—an entirely
new way to live."

The second dynamic of this verse tells how he pro-
poses to impart this precious gift. He offers an exchange
of yokes. To people under a yoke he offers a new yoke.
Instead of the yoke of heavy burden, he offers his own
yoke of freedom. We need to think about that. Two trib-
utaries of ancient parlance and practice flow together to
form a vivid image of what the yoke means. The rabbis
of the time spoke of a yoke relationship of a student with
his teacher. The word *yoke* was a synonym for school.
This is surely part of what Jesus meant, for he followed
his challenge to take his yoke with the invitation to learn
of him. Further, investigation into the eastern methods
of plowing helps us to understand what Jesus meant by
the yoke. Mosaic law forbade an old and a young ox to
be yoked together with an ordinary yoke. This was because the young animal could not pull his part of the
burden. The phrase "unequally yoked" comes from this.
A training yoke was required by law. The heavy end of
the yoke was the burden of the stronger, older beast. It

was placed at the end of the furrow. It kept the furrow straight and, under the reigns of the plowman, moved forward. All the younger beast had to do was to keep parallel with the stronger animal. If it pulled away, ahead, or behind, its neck would be rubbed raw in the yoke. The trainee had to give up the right to lead in order to keep pace with the trainer. The lead ox must take the lead and the responsibility for the burden. Now it begins to dawn on us what Christ meant when he offered us the yoke as a source of freedom.

Our minds leap to the implication. Christ carries the heavy end of the yoke. He pulls the burden for us. We must give up our wills to him. Patience is developed in the school of Christ. We are yoked with him to discover how to live with his guidance, strategy, and timing. Impatience is running ahead, pulling off in our own direction, or lagging behind in petulant pouting. Patience is developed through a parallel pace with the Master. The cadences of his perfect will in our lives and in other people we love sets the rhythm of a life of peace.

We all know what it is like to be rubbed raw through our own impatience. We have all tried to accomplish our goals on our own strength; and equally defeating, we have tried to do his work on our strength. It will not work. We become impatient when we want to do what we want when we want it and with whom we want it. Who has not bashed down a closed door while an open door stood open, with the Master inviting us to follow him inside?

To be in a training yoke with Christ means several magnificent gifts are offered to us. He carries the burden! We were never created to live the Christian life on our own. The source of our strength is in surrendering our burdens to him. As soon as we are yoked with Christ, the load is lifted. All we have to do is keep pace. Bernard of Clairvaux explained that such a yoke is a blessed burden that makes all burdens light, a yoke that bears the bearer up.

In the yoke with Christ, we can give up the responsibility of running the universe. We can have intimate communion with the Lord at all times. Our times are in God's hands. He knows what he is doing. When was the last time you told him you knew that and completely gave up the direction, desires, and duration of your life's furrow? Patience is the fruit of that yoke union. Thomas à Kempis said that if we wanted to be free to enjoy our own will, then we would never be peaceful or free from care. Impatience really is breaking the first commandment. It is making ourselves a god over our own lives. It does not work. It has not since the beginning of time.

Being a yokefellow with Christ assures us of guidance and direction. If we ask him, and abide in him until the answer becomes clear, we will feel release from tension. We will not panic. The Lord who gives each day will show the way.

That is what he means when he says, "My yoke is easy and my burden light." The word for "easy" is *chrestos* in the Greek text. It means kindly, a divine offer. At that time, the word *kindness* was used only for God. Jesus as the Messiah, the I Am, was the only one who could make such an offer. Kindness implies empathy and understanding, forgiveness, and a constant flow of second chances. God is ultimately kind to us, and that kindness was manifested in his Son's life and sacrificial death. Jesus is telling us that to be yoked with him is an experience of a continuous flow of kindness. That enables true patience, first with ourselves, then with our inept shortcomings, and then with others and their failures and inability to meet our standards.

But also note the further assurance of the way that Jesus helps us when we are yoked to him. His burden is light. That can mean either that we have the light end of the training yoke, or that as he carries the heavier end of the yoke, he is yoked with God himself. During his ministry, Jesus exemplified the quality of dependent trust in God which he wanted his followers to emulate. His constant and consistent communion with God in times of prayer and repeated relinquishment gives the secret of the right balance of divine discontent and trust in the Lord's final justice and grace.

The third aspect of this verse is focused in what Jesus teaches us while we are yoked to him. He tells us that he is "gentle and lowly in heart." The King James version of the Bible renders it "meek and lowly." The word means leadable, open to be guided, teachable, receptive. One of the uses of the word *meek* was for an animal which had been broken and would follow the lead of the reins. An impatient person is the opposite of this. Impatience is bucking, refusing to be guided, and taking things into our own control. It is demanding that things go our way, on our schedule, regardless of the cost.

The fourth aspect of Christ's salient secret for the cure of impatience is that the yoke of Christ provides rest for our souls. The Lord promised that if we become yokefellows with him we would need consistent times of rest. As the leader of our yoked training with him, he will not only lead the way and determine the pace, but he will also know when to stop us in our tracks. The word *rest* in this verse means refreshment. The Lord refreshes us by renewing our inner conviction that he is the source of our wisdom, guidance, and strategic timing. It is when we are quiet that we know that he is able to do all things well and is worthy of our trust.

Years ago, philosopher William Ernest Hocking, in his classic, *The Meaning of God in Human Experience,* elucidated what he called the "principles of alternation." We need times of rest to regain our perspective and power. When we go without deliberate pauses, we begin to get in our own way, and thus we defeat our own work. I know this is true from my own experience. I am most impatient when I am overtired, spiritually exhausted, or emotionally drained. Since the major cause of impatience with others and circumstances is impatience with ourselves, we need times when we allow God to heal our depleted self-esteem and renew our delight in being the unique miracle God created us to be.

A busy physician once told me that he was going off for a week of silence on a retreat. "I need to fall in love again—with the Lord, myself, people, and life, in that order!" Not a bad prescription for healing impatience. In the clamorous din around us and in us, we need to listen again to the voice of gentle stillness.

Leonardo da Vinci was asked why he had long periods of inactivity while he was painting *The Last Supper.* He said that when he paused the longest, it was then that he made the most telling strokes with his brush. The same is true for us. We require quiet intervals if we are to win the battle with impatience. It may seem strange to you that quiet, prayerful inactivity and meditation would help impatience. Why not get on with it, get at the task and finish it? The problem is that tension mounts, and we become ineffective.

The Lord told the psalmist, "Be still and know that I am God." When the psalmist followed the Lord's directive, he was able finally to write the admonition, "Wait on the Lord: be of good courage, and he shall strengthen thine heart: wait, I say, on the Lord" (Psalm 27:14, KJV). "My soul, wait thou only upon God; for my expectation is from him" (Psalm 62:5, KJV). Note the progression: wait, receive courage, and go forward with strength. Without resting in the Lord, our impatience causes impetuousness. Our greatest errors and strained relationships come when we have lost touch with the Lord's inner guidance and wisdom. Frederick W. Faber once said that we must wait for God. We must wait long, meekly, in wind and wet, in the thunder and lightning, in the cold and the dark. We must wait, and he will come. But God never comes to those who do not wait.

It is in the waiting times that our most creative thoughts and plans are formulated. Instead of rushing headlong in our own impatience, the Lord is able to tell us what are the next steps and how we are to move forward in his strategy for us and the people around us.

When Dante appeared at the Franciscan monastery door, a monk opened the door and asked him what he wanted. "Peace!" was Dante's one word answer. That eventually became the Lord's gift to him when he learned to wait, pray, and listen. Later, in *The Divine Comedy*, he wrote his oft-quoted line, "In His will is our peace." The refreshment of Christ is peace to replace our impatience. Then we can pray with Richard of Chichester, the thirteenth-century saint,

> O most merciful Redeemer, Friend
> and Brother, may we know Thee
> more clearly, love Thee more dearly,
> and follow Thee more nearly; for
> Thine own sake.—Amen.

Christ is peace. Christ is patience. We could never produce these graces in our own strength in the quantities they are needed in our families and our world. But we do have access to an unlimited stockpile of patience because the same Spirit that enabled Christ is in us.

8

How to Get up
When You're Down
on Yourself

DO YOU EVER get down on yourself? It happens to all
of us at times. We feel it when we do not measure up to
our own standards. It attacks when we have failed to do
what we had planned or compulsively repeat old habits
we thought we had left behind. Our accomplishments do
not match our expectations. Dreams are unfulfilled,
hopes are dashed, and agendas are tardy. Who is to
blame? "It is I!" we say to ourselves. The "if onlys" of the
past invade the "what ifs" of the present. We are en-
gulfed in a sense of guilt. "If I had been different, if I
had worked harder, if I had been wiser, if I had been
stronger," becomes the dirge of self-incrimination.

We all have an awesome capacity of self-scrutiny.
We can analyze our own performance and personalities.
Coupled with that is our capacity to remember. We are
haunted by old memories of what we did that we should
not have done and what we should have done that we

never accomplished. It is then that we become our own parents, or our own diminutive god, and take over the punishment of ourselves. Discouragement and depression result. Our conscience shakes an accusing finger.

Self-condemnation sets in. Self-esteem drains out. We begin to feel bad about ourselves. Self-negation dominates our feelings. It is then that we become most vulnerable to do what we promised ourselves we would never do. We act out our depleted self-image. Others are treated the way we treat ourselves. We become unkind in word and action. Our sense of guilt thrashes about searching for something to do which will support its negative self-appraisal—all so we can say, "See, what you did is what you are!"

It is difficult to get up for life when we are down on ourselves. What can we do about our sense of guilt, self-negation, and resultant self-condemnation? What would it take to give us a whole new picture of ourselves as loved and lovable, forgiven and forgiving?

I talked to a man who was down on himself. After he had told me all the things he could muster up to support his bad feelings about himself, he said a stunning thing, "If I could only forget the failures and remember the accomplishments, I'd be okay. I've got a good memory and a poor forgetter."

A poor forgetter! The word is not in the dictionary. It should be. Allow me to venture a definition. A "forgetter" is the capacity to forget the failures and inadequacies of the past. What we remember and what we forget is crucial for our spiritual and mental health. The only way to get up when we are down on ourselves is to have our memories healed and our forgetters strengthened.

The great French philosopher Henri Bergson said

that it is the function of the brain to make us not only to remember but to forget. We laugh. "I must have a super brain because of all the things I forget!" we say. Who has not forgotten someone's birthday or an important date on our calendars. We do not need training in forgetfulness. We are highly trained experts in that! But why is it that we forget things we want to remember and remember things we long to forget? Why is it that one failure sticks in our memory and hundreds of achievements are forgotten? There are lots of training courses available for memory training. I have never seen one on how to forget. And yet our inability to forget gives our compulsive conscience lots of accusing ammunition. We need help in developing our "forgetter."

But we cannot do that for ourselves. We are immobilized by our feeling of guilt. Others cannot help us. They are either too down on themselves to help or too glib in their encouraging affirmations to be taken seriously. It does not help for someone to tell us we are great if we feel gross. Their accolades are dismissed by our incriminating self. "If they only knew! They wouldn't be so magnanimous."

A healthy forgetter is developed by forgiveness. We cannot erase the memory cards of our failures in our brain computer until we have a profound experience of forgiveness. The authentic mark of truly mature persons is the capacity to forgive themselves. But that is a rare commodity. Years of experience of seeking to be a whole person and helping others with their self-esteem has led me to the conclusion that one of the greatest miracles of life is self-forgiveness. I have never known a person who has been able to do it without a healing experience of Christ's kindness.

The purpose of this chapter is to plumb the depths

of self-condemnation and to show how Christ's kindness can help us to get up when we are down on ourselves. His kindness for us enables a kindness in us for ourselves, and then for others. The fruit of the Spirit is kindness.

Kindness is the steadfast love of the Lord in action toward those who fail. Throughout the Old Testament the words for steadfast love, mercy, and kindness are used interchangeably. "Let him who glories glory in this, that he understands and knows me, that I am the Lord who practice steadfast love" (Jeremiah 9:24). The American Standard Bible translates it "lovingkindness." Kindness is the persistent effort of the Lord to reach his people and enable them to return to him.

Jesus Christ was kindness incarnate. He came to express it; lived to model it; died to offer it; and returns in the Holy Spirit to impart it to us. Paul knew this from his own experience of the kindness of God in Christ. His rigid hostility toward others and himself had been melted by an unsurpassed kindness. The new creation in the apostle Paul was expressed in kindness. The Lord's call for kindness in his people through the prophet Micah was now possible. God never demands anything of us that he is not willing to give us. It should not be surprising that the power to be kind is available under the code name *fruit*. Kindness is implanted, imputed, and ingrained into the very nature of our new heredity in Christ Jesus. It is ours to develop and express along with the other character strengths inherent in the fruit of the Spirit. Kindness can now be reflected in all our relationships. We can be as merciful and gracious to others as Christ has been to us.

There is no encounter in scripture which is more revealing of the kindness of Christ than the account of the woman caught in adultery (John 7:53—8:11). What happened to the woman exemplifies what occurs when the kindness of Christ penetrates the dark places of hidden memories and remorse.

Put yourself in the scene. We are there in the crowd listening to the Master teach in the precincts of the Temple. Suddenly his teaching is interrupted by the jeers and frenzied cries of a crowd which approaches. A ghastly procession breaks through the crowd around Jesus. It is led by scribes and Pharisees. An angry, bloodthirsty mob follows close behind. Though the woman offers no resistance, they push her down before Jesus. She writhes in anguished sobs. What charge deserves this kind of treatment? It is obvious that she is no woman of the streets, no sensuous enticer of men's affections for a price. There is a dignity which has been crushed by this cruelty, a discernible longing which has been twisted and maligned.

Our hearts ache for the woman. We feel a combination of embarrassment and shock. Our own hidden thoughts and memories are jabbed awake. Who has not had fantasies and feelings, if not actual failures, which if exposed would put us at Jesus' feet?

We look into the fiendishly frenzied faces of the scribes and Pharisees. Condemnation oozes from every pore of their faces. Then our eyes fall on their hands. In each one is a large stone. They are ready to stone the woman! What crime deserves this? But we know the answer.

The scribes and Pharisees confirm our suspicions. "Teacher!" they say, addressing Jesus in supercilious mockery of his sacred title, "This woman has been caught in the act of adultery." Their voices grow in self-righteous intensity. "Now in the law Moses commanded us to stone such. What do you say about her?" Our minds leap back to the ancient scriptures. We think of Leviticus 20:10, "If a man commits adultery with the wife of his neighbor, both the adulterer and the adulteress shall be put to death." The woman does not have a chance!

We look at her, crumpled and broken, before Jesus. How do we feel about that charge? Questions begin to surge into our minds. Where is the man if the woman was taken in the *very* act? Wasn't he equally guilty? And how did the scribes and Pharisees find her in her adulterous act? Could it have been staged? Is it possible that one of those who holds a stone enticed her into the compromising indiscretion so the leaders could present Jesus with an impossible decision? But what was it that motivated the angry condemnation of these leaders? Suddenly it dawns on us that they would have to have been down on themselves before they could make such a vitriolic attack on this woman. There is so much more than meets the eye here. These men are more hostile toward Jesus than they are the woman! Could it be that he has put a finger on a raw nerve in them through his teaching and preaching? Were they convicted before they convicted the woman?

Jesus is confronted with an impossible dilemma. If he denies the Law, he might be stoned himself. If he sanctions the execution of the woman, he will be going against Rome which has forbidden capital punishment by the Jews and their courts. There seems to be no way out. The condemning leaders have used a human being as a thing to trap him. Jesus has gained the reputation of being a friend to sinners. Will this force him to deny his compassionate ministry? We watch him closely to observe what he will do.

We are deeply moved by the look on his face. He

stares into the faces of the angry mob and then down on the woman at his feet. She is too ashamed to lift her head.

Then deliberately he stoops down. He lowers his head. What is he doing? The silence is alarming. We all wait with bated breath.

With majestic authority he raises his hand, his forefinger protruding with royal dignity. All eyes are immediately focused on that regal finger. Will he use it to point accusingly at the woman, the leaders, or us? Instead, he slowly, deliberately begins to write in the dusty sand of the ground. We strain our necks to see what he is writing. We cannot see closely enough to discern it.

The leaders did not want to know. One and then another begins to jibe and press him in demanding tones. The crowd picks up the chant. "Give us an answer. The woman's guilty! Make your judgment!"

Jesus straightens to full height. Fire flashes from his eyes like lightning. The thunder of his voice follows quickly. It hits us like a blow. "Let him who is without sin among you be the first to throw a stone at her." A murmur of uneasiness grips the crowd. They had not expected that. The tables have turned. Those who had wanted to trap Jesus now are the ones who feel trapped.

Once again Jesus stops to write in the sand. What is he writing? It must be convicting, whatever it is, because the leaders suddenly have panicked looks on their faces. They look at each other with an expression that expresses a frightened, "How did he know?" The Lord must be writing the commandments or the hidden sins he discerned in these condemnatory leaders. Or could it be that he is writing the Hebrew word *hesed,* reminding the people of the mercy of God.

Silence again. No one is moving a muscle. And then

the silence is broken by a thud of a large stone on the ground. We observe that the eldest of the Pharisees has dropped his stone. His judgment-worn face is twisted. But now the hard lines of indignant superiority are softened a bit. Then there is another thud, and then another. The carefully selected, sharp, and craggy stones begin to rain down at the feet of the accusing, judgmental critics. The woman cringes, expecting each one to hit her in judgment for her crime. She lifts her head in amazement as the leaders turn away, some in shame; others in grumbling defeat; others in retreat to find another chance to attack Jesus. From the eldest to the youngest, we want to leave also. Nasty business, this! We feel anguish for the woman and anxiety for ourselves. We want to get out of there before Jesus writes our hidden sins upon the ground or reminds us of our merciless attitude toward ourselves or toward someone like this woman.

We walk away hoping not to be noticed. And then we glance back to observe the tenderest encounter we have ever seen. Jesus is still stooping, his finger in the sand. The broken woman looks up and her eyes meet his. Kindness radiates from his face. He stands up with measured movements and lifts the woman up until they are face to face. We can hear what he says. An awesome pity and a pitiful person meet. "Woman, where are they? Has no one condemned you?"

The woman looks around in amazement. "No one, Lord." It is as if Jesus wants to underline the fact that she is free of her accusers. But now, what about her own attitude toward herself? Will she be able to forget and make a new beginning?

His words of comfort and assurance are the most

compassionate and authoritative ever spoken to anyone. We feel the impact of them as we listen. We are there in the woman's place. He takes us by the shoulders, looks deeply into our eyes and says, "Neither do I condemn you; go, and do not sin again."

Amazing! The sin is not condoned. But there is no condemnation. Kindness affording the power to forget.

We are left to ponder what this means for us. We find ourselves in the skin of the accusers and the accused. Our unresolved guilt has caused us to act like those scribes and Pharisees more often than we want to remember. Our religion has prompted more condemnation than culpability. The more uneasy we are about our past, the more we get down on ourselves, and eventually we become arrogant, religious prigs whose insecurity is expressed by being down on others. But we are also forced to find ourselves at Jesus' feet, guilty as charged. No one has thrown us there. We have thrust ourselves there by our own self-condemnation. And the only hope of getting up from being down on ourselves is found in his words. Do you hear his kindness in your own soul? "Neither do I condemn you. Go and sin no more!"

We wonder what happened to the woman and her accusers after this confrontation of the destructive power of condemnation. Did the Pharisees and scribes become more kind? Perhaps some of them realized that their own feeling of guilt under the impact of Jesus' ministry had prompted them to be severe in their judgment of the woman. We would like to think that they began a new life of kindness toward others because of Jesus' writing in the ground. But history testifies that as a group, they never allowed the experience to affect their hearts or be expressed in their behavior. They continued with condemnation until they impaled Jesus not only on the horns of a dilemma but on a cross. Religious judgmentalism dies hard, and is too seldom cured.

If we find ourselves among the accusers in this dramatic story, we have some painful questions to ask.

1. Do we ever escape our own self-condemnation by a critical, negative spirit to others?
2. Do we project onto others our own weary sense of guilt?
3. Do we expose and malign others for sins and failures we find in ourselves?
4. Do we hold others at a distance until they measure up?
5. Do we play god by meting out judgments and demanding that people atone to us for what they have done or been?
6. Have we been as merciful and gracious to others as our Lord has been to us?

But many of us find ourselves in the woman. Not only do we feel accused, but we accuse ourselves. Our failure may not be as obvious or easily categorized as the woman's, but what we are and have done is no less serious to our Lord.

To feel the full impact of the woman's plight and how Jesus dealt with her, we need to single out whatever it is that makes us feel down on ourselves right now. What is it for you? Whether it is great or small, it is the roadblock to healthy self-acceptance and self-esteem. Think about that as we grapple with how Jesus helps us to get up when we are down on ourselves.

Whatever the syndrome of loneliness or longing, the woman ended up more down on herself than the scribes and Pharisees could ever be. They only articulated what she already felt about herself. Their enacted exposure and judgment was nothing in comparison to what she had done to herself in her own mind a thousand times before. She had rendered the guilty charge on herself long before she was thrown at the feet of the Master.

The woman's own self-condemnation concerns the Lord most in this story. Once he got rid of the would-be accusers, he had to deal with the most vigilant accuser of all—the person inside the woman. Until she was as kind to herself as he was, she would not be free to live a new life. She had to change her mind about herself. Three things had to be accomplished. She needed radical forgiveness, remedial forgetfulness, and releasing freedom. And Jesus provided all three.

Radical forgiveness enables us to forgive ourselves. That can happen only if someone with an ultimate authority forgives us. Simply to forgive ourselves without the experience of forgiveness from another does not work. Jesus Christ has the authority and the power to forgive.

We have developed a lot of fancy words for our failures. Maladjustment, neurosis, complexes, need satisfaction, or emotional sickness. But only one word defines our condition—*sin*, separation from the Lord. Our deepest need is for reconciliation and relationship with him. We are sinners. Our actions habitually break God's law for what he meant us to be. The Ten Commandments and Jesus' great commandment to love the Lord our God with all our mind, soul, and body have not gone out of style.

Forgiveness gives us the hope of forgetting what is behind and moving on to live. We all long for that more than anything else. Louisa Fletcher Tarkington expresses how we all feel:

I wish that there were some wonderful place
  In the Land of Beginning Again:
Where all our mistakes and all our heartaches
  And all of our poor selfish grief
Could be dropped like a shabby old coat at the door
  And never put on again.

The land of beginning again is here and now. Jesus stands at the door welcoming us home from wherever we have wandered. This is the basis of remedial forgetfulness. We wonder what happened to the woman after she parted from the Master that day. Did she continue to condemn herself? Could she forget? Only if she could remember Jesus' words of kindness more than she remembered her sin. Robert Louis Stevenson said that it is our friends who stand between us and our self-contempt. And only Jesus can be that kind of friend who can close the door of the past and keep us from wandering furtively down the corridors of debilitating memory.

The central hope of the Christian faith is that we are new creatures in Christ—the old can pass away, the new can come! Listen to Paul who had a great deal which could haunt him. "Forgetting what lies behind and straining forward to what lies ahead, I press on toward the goal for the prize of the upward call of God in Christ Jesus" (Philippians 3:13-14). That is why he could say, "From now on, therefore, we regard no one from a human point of view; even though we regarded Christ from a human point of view we regard him thus no longer" (2 Corinthians 5:16). What the apostle meant was that he no longer thought of Christ as one man among many. "God was in Christ reconciling the world" (2 Corinthians 5:19). On that basis we no longer regard ourselves or others from the human perspective of judgment and condemnation. We are forgiven and released to forget. "Therefore, if any one is in Christ, he is a new creation; the old has passed away, behold, the new has come. All this is from God, who through Christ reconciled us to himself and gave us the ministry of reconciliation" (2 Corinthians 5:17-18). And that ministry of reconciliation begins with our own reconciliation to ourselves.

Only Christianity offers that. What a contrast with Mohammed who said in the Koran that every man's fate is fastened about his neck and he is accountant against himself. Not so with Christ. Christ has taken the sin and written "paid in full" across the ledger sheet of besetting memories.

The same capacity of the brain which we use to remember can be used to remember to forget. Each time the memory of our failure invades our consciousness and attacks our peace, we can recapture the experience of the kindness of our Lord and our forgiveness.

I overheard some friends say to a woman who had been through a lot, "Don't you remember all the tragedies of the past?" Her response was, "No, all I remember is the day I decided to forget."

The only memories which have any power to stalk our present thoughts are those which have never been forgiven. If you have such memories, do battle with them right now. Look them in the face and then tell the Lord about what you did or said. He lived and died for us, and he has forgiven us. We can sing with the psalmist, "As the heavens are high above the earth, so great is his steadfast love toward those who fear him; as far as the east is from the west, so far does he remove our transgressions from us" (Psalm 103:11-12).

Can we dare to say, "I can't forgive myself," if our

Lord who created us and saved us has said, "I forgive you"? The ultimate blasphemy and the most disastrous arrogance is to be less to ourselves than God has been.

Speak to yourself now in the quiet of your own heart. Say your name. "_____, I forgive you as one forgiven by the Lord."

Now we are ready for a releasing freedom. Jesus did more than forgive the woman. He told her to go and sin no more. How would she accomplish that? Only if her self-condemnatory spirit had been healed by the Lord's forgiving spirit.

Paul said, "For freedom Christ has set us free; stand fast therefore, and do not submit again to a yoke of slavery" (Galatians 5:1). The new yoke of slavery is offered every day by life's temptations and challenges. How can we be free?

We do what we do because of what we are inside. Until those needs are met creatively we will be vulnerable constantly. We all need a new image of ourselves, Christ's picture of us, a portrait of a loved and accepted person. Until his love possesses and pervades us, we will seek to use people and things as substitutes.

The sure test that we have accepted the Lord's image of us as forgiven is that we begin to feel good about ourselves. A new dignity and self-worth replaces the negative self-depreciation; self-hate is the prelude to all the things we do which cause us to despise ourselves. The formula works. Allow Christ to love you; dare to love yourself as an accepted, forgiven person. Jesus is more concerned about our reclamation than recrimination.

Now is the only moment we have. It is the first moment of our new future. Start where you stand!

There is a lovely story of a man who asked an older

man in a little village what the seemingly insignificant wide place in the road was known for. "Young man," the villager responded, "this is the starting place for any place in the world. You can start from here and go anywhere you want to."

In a way that is what Jesus Christ says to us right now. Feel his strong arms lift you up when you are down on yourself. "Neither do I condemn you. Go and sin no more!" That is all we need to know. We are forgiven, free to forget, and released to live without self-condemnation. The fruit of the kindness of God will be manifested in kindness to others.

9

For Goodness Sake!

A FEW YEARS ago I conducted the funeral of a very outstanding man. The hearse pulled up beside the burial place, and I took my place along with the pallbearers to lead the procession. As we moved along past the gravestones, I was deeply engrossed in the meaning of the service.

I felt the loss of this man who had been a part of the strategy of God in the lives of many people because the power of God had been at work in his own life. Reflecting on this, I was shocked by the arrogant words of an old tombstone beside the path marking the grave of a man buried years before. I almost stopped in my tracks.

What kind of a man would have that kind of a gravestone with that kind of an epitaph? Chiseled in granite were these words: "Here lies a man who had what it takes."

What it takes for what? To live a full and abundant

life? To be a success? To be powerful? To live a rich and creative life that makes a difference? To be a good person? Did God agree that the man·represented by that gravestone had what it takes?

I talked to a woman who was deeply depressed. She had had a very difficult life. Her husband had left her and later came back for a weekend. During the visit he had secretly packed the children's clothes, and, when she was away at the grocery store, he took the children. She had no way of knowing where they were. She looked at me with tears streaming down her face and said, "Lloyd, I just don't have what it takes!"

A man wrote me about an awesome challenge he had been given. The opportunity was immense. He felt inadequate and insecure. In the letter he confessed, "If I were only good enough and had what it takes!"

If we are to do what it takes and have what it takes, it will mean that we allow God to work his very nature into the fabric of our character. It is his plan to do this. He is ready to implant his spirit into the very substance of our personalities. We have discussed the resulting character traits of love, joy, peace, patience, kindness. We are ready now to talk about goodness.

The fruit of the Spirit is goodness.

What does it mean to be a good person? What is Sammy's mother asking of her son when she says, "Sammy, you be a good boy!"

The meaning of the word *good* is that which a thing is—sufficient for its purpose in and of itself without any admixtures. When we say, "That was a good song," we mean that it was faithful to the laws of music. Its form was well thought through, and it was performed impeccably. When we say a person is a good person, we mean that he or she has fulfilled the purpose of being a person—able to receive love and give love.

Most people's notion of goodness is related to agreeable behavior or flawless morality. God's idea of goodness is concerned with something much more than that. When he created the world and all of the aspects of it, he reviewed his work and concluded, "It is good." At the end of the sixth day of creation he formed a human being, and then he said, "It is very good."

In the Hebrew text there is nothing uncomplicated about the use of the word *good* in this passage. It means that all of the aspects of creation are ready and able to fulfill their purpose. The plant life, the seas, the fish that swim in the seas, the animals that roam the plains, and the supreme and sublime level of his creation, human beings, are all able to function as they were intended. All are good.

Now all of creation is to be a glory to God and a manifestation of his power. Our essential purpose in creation is to glorify God and enjoy him forever. Insofar as "all creatures great and small" keep a life consistent with the basic reason for which they exist, goodness is maintained.

Adam and Eve did not lose their "good" rating with God just because they did a lot of bad things. Evil entered into history when they said no to their Maker. They did so by refusing to be faithful to the conditions of obedience which were dramatized or symbolized for them in a tree at the center of Eden's garden. The evil mirrored in their act was their refusal to be what they were intended to be in relationship to God.

God brooded over his flawed creation. He sought out a plan to bring humankind back to what God had intended—good, open to God, a channel of his own grace, building lives, relationships, society, and the kingdom of God according to the purpose for which humankind was created.

To enlarge our understanding of the meaning of goodness, let's look at some biblical passages that deal with the goodness of God as it was observable to humanity. It will also help us understand the goodness potential made available to us in the fruit of the Spirit.

Psalm 27 records David's prayer in the midst of difficult circumstances. His enemies were all around him. His family and friends had denied him. But those circumstantial facts are quite secondary in David's focus. He said, "I believe that I shall see the goodness of the Lord in the land of the living! Wait for the Lord; be strong, and let your heart take courage; yea, wait for the Lord!" (Psalm 27:13-14).

David knew that God was good in spite of the fact that David's enemies were bad. He trusted God—God's consistency, God's integrity, and God's authenticity. And that is what it means to be good. Some of the greatest persons of history show evidences of being both bad and good. But we see the goodness of God flash through at various times, not because the people lived perfect lives, but because they allowed God to work through them.

Look at Psalm 65. Here again the goodness of God was experienced because he was able to bring persons he made in his image back to what he intended their lives to be. "Blessed is he whom thou dost choose and bring near, to dwell in thy courts! We shall be satisfied with the goodness of thy house, thy holy temple!" (Psalm 65:4).

It is Jeremiah who gives us the key verse about the goodness of God, and it is recorded in the twelfth verse of chapter 31. He says: "They shall be radiant over the goodness of the Lord."

When we feel that God is good—good to us in spite of everything we have said and done—then we know that mercy takes the shape of goodness. God's goodness is that he knows our need even before we ask him. God's goodness is that he goes before us to show the way. God's goodness was that at the time humankind deserved it least, he came in Jesus Christ to reveal himself and to die for the sins of the whole race. He came to make men and women good from inside.

Goodness is an inside story. We are made good not by our efforts but by the efficacy of the atonement accomplished by Jesus Christ on the cross. Our status before God is in and through Christ. He accepts us as new creatures, made good on Calvary. We could not dare to come to God apart from the imputed goodness of our vicarious standing through the Savior. The Lord looks at us through the focused lens of Calvary. Our confidence is not in our human facsimilies of goodness, but in our relationship with Christ. We are freed from compulsive efforts to be good enough to deserve love. Instead we can live in the settled security of goodness in Christ.

Paul confronts this issue in Romans. He quotes portions of Psalm 14 and 53 in establishing what we are like apart from Christ. "None is righteous, no, not one; no one understands, no one seeks for God. All have turned aside, together they have gone wrong; no one does good, not even one" (Romans 3:10-12). The apostle goes on to assert that no one will be justified, made good, by works. Then he thunders the essential truth. "But now the righteousness of God has been manifested apart from law, although the law and the prophets bear witness to it, the righteousness of God through faith in Jesus Christ for all who believe" (Romans 3:21-22). To be sure we get the point that our goodness is in Christ, Paul restates the case. "For there is no distinction; since all have sinned and fall short of the glory of God, they are justified by his grace as a gift, through the redemption which is in Christ Jesus, whom God put forward as an expiation by his blood, to be received by faith" (Romans 3:22-24).

Our goodness in Christ is a gift. We accept it by faith and then are released to live in the flow of his goodness through us. On the basis of that we can respond to Paul's challenge to "overcome evil with good" (Romans 12:21). And that is possible because our life will be guided by the Lord in each situation and relationship.

> I appeal to you therefore, brethren, by the mercies of God, to present your bodies as a living sacrifice, holy and acceptable to God, which is your spiritual worship. Do not be conformed to this world but be transformed by the renewal of your mind, that you may prove what is the will of God, what is good and acceptable and perfect.
>
> ROMANS 12:1-2

After we have worked through the concept of goodness as a gift accepted by faith, so many of Paul's admonitions come alive with fresh impact. Based on the fruit of goodness through our redemption and Christ's spirit in us, we can be "of good courage" (2 Corinthians 5:8), know that we were re-created in Christ "for good works" (Ephesians 2:10), render service with "good will" (Ephesians 6:7), bear fruit in "every good work" (2 Corinthians 9:8), "hold fast what is good" (1 Thessalonians 5:21), have a "good conscience" (1 Timothy 1:5), be a "good minister of Christ" (1 Timothy 4:6), "fight the good fight of the faith" (1 Timothy 6:12), and "be equipped for every good work" (2 Timothy 3:17). All the good things we should do and say will flow from the headwaters of Christ's goodness in us. We will have what Whitehead called an "habitual vision of greatness."

The Lord gets inside of us. He takes the tangled mess of our memories of what we have done or said that we never should have done or said. And he takes all the confused relationships, the fantasies and the fears, and he forgives them. He deals redemptively with our guilt and cleanses and heals us because he is good—and he created us to be good.

So our notion that goodness is obtained by a pietistic withdrawal from ungodly persons for fear of contamination is false. Our admonitions to people, "Try and be good," and eulogies like, "Here was a really good person," are comforting but usually wide of the mark of true goodness. Christ-imputed goodness can be attributed only to someone who trusts him and is filled with his spirit, to someone who dares in all things to trust God for direction, guidance, and the impartation of his own nature.

The church fathers put it this way: "God is a Spirit, infinite, eternal, and unchangeable, in his being (in his essential nature), wisdom, power, holiness, justice, goodness, and truth" (The Shorter Catechism).

It is possible to treasure such a profound declaration to the point that it becomes a revered document instead of a truth to be realized and appropriated. God wants to make us like himself. When the Holy Spirit takes residence in us, he makes us consistent, authentic, real persons. We become good and are able to see the right and do it, motivated by his love. We sense the needs of others, and without being told, we respond with mercy.

God has been good to us so that we may be good

people. His goodness in us can be constant, but opportunities to share it are fleeting and unrepeatable. It was Etienne de Grellet who put it this way:

> I shall pass through this world but once. If, therefore, there be any kindness I can show, or any good thing I can do, let me do it now; let me not defer it or neglect it, for I shall not pass this way again.

Even now, in the quiet, do you feel it? Do you sense it? God has declared you good in Jesus Christ. His own nature has been implanted in you. Have you ever thought of the wonder of being shaped in the image of Christ? He longs to live his life, develop his character, and love his world through you. Inadvertently, winsomely, naturally, freely—his goodness will grow in you and become part of your own character. Hugh Latimer was right: "We must first be made good before we can do good." Goodness is not just what we do but the inward thing we become through the reconciliation of the cross and the infilling of the fruit of the Spirit.

Then we can say with the psalmist, "Surely goodness and mercy shall follow me all the days of my life." I have often wondered why he said "follow me." Could it be that he meant that the Lord takes care of the enemies which attack us from behind? There are enemies of our yesterdays which can attack and rob us of our birthright of goodness in the present. Memories dog our steps. Past sins are forever on our heels. We move forward, but the relentless fears of the past persist. But then the Lord becomes our rear guard as well as our advance guard. We know we will "dwell in the house of the Lord for ever," and we also know that the Lord's "goodness and mercy" stand between us and our yesterdays. He is Lord of the past and Lord of the future so that we can enjoy the "goodness" of companionship with him today.

I am gratified that when I got by the "Here lies a man who had what it takes" tombstone, I led the procession on to the open grave of the dear friend I was burying that day. We committed his body to the ground with the full assurance that he was alive in the house of the Lord. When the grave was closed, his marker was put in place. It gave his name, the years of his physical life on earth, and these powerful words, "To God be the glory." That is all a good person ever needs to say about yesterday, tomorrow, and today!

10

The Amazing Resources of God

THE CROWDS SWIRLED around the Master. He was back in Cana of Galilee after his visit to Jerusalem where he had cleansed the temple, driving out the money changers. News of that had traveled far and wide. His new fame, the mighty acts he performed, and his transformation of water into wine a short time before made him the man of the hour. He received a hero's welcome.

The people surrounded him with buzzing excitement. They pressed in upon him with provincial enthusiasm for one of their own countrymen who had become the talk of Israel. Local pride brought people flocking to him. What would he do next? What sign or wonder would astound them further?

We look into Jesus' face—sadness. The faithless people wanted more signs and not the word he wanted to give about God's love and the kingdom. He looked at the people, longing to touch the deeper need in them with the miracle of God's faithfulness. But they did not recognize either who he really was or what miracle he could perform in their souls.

Then suddenly, a wave of amazement rippled over the crowd. A royal official in high standing in Herod's court had entered the edge of the crowd. He had traveled the twenty miles from Capernaum to see Jesus.

The crowd parted with solicitous deference, making a passage corridor for the courtier to come face to face with Jesus. The Master turned his attention from the crowd to meet the man.

It was obvious that the otherwise contained and sufficient official was distraught. Nothing could stop him. Single-minded determination pressed him through the crowd. The Lord, responding to authentic human need, greeted him tenderly and asked him to speak.

With urgency mingled with pathos, the man sobbed and told his plight. "My son is at the point of death with a burning fever. News of your mighty acts has reached us at Capernaum. Come down and heal my son!"

The crowd around Jesus responded with expectancy. Surley the Lord would go with him immediately to heal the boy. One more sign and wonder for the thrill-hungry but faithless crowd.

Again, a sadness descended over Jesus' face. He looked away from the courtier to the frenzied people cheering for a new miracle. "Unless you see signs and wonders you will not believe," he said firmly, pointedly (John 4:48). The word was spoken to the crowd, not to the nobleman, for the verb forms are plural.

The anguished, worried parent was persistent. His mind was on nothing but his son who was dying. "Sir, come down before my child dies!" he cried out pathetically and urgently (John 4:49).

110

The Master turned again to him. His face brightened. His countenance was radiant, and his voice was filled with divine authority. "Go; your son will live" (4:50). The air was filled with hope. The courtier looked into Jesus' eyes, and as he gazed, something happened inside of him. Faith was born. Trust in the Master's words flowed with surging power in his soul. The longer he looked into Jesus' face, the more confident he became. A peace flushed over him, and he realized his son was well. In the presence of the Lord, he knew that his request had been answered. Joy leaped up inside of him. He could not wait to get back to Capernaum to see for himself and hold his healed son in his arms.

There are few verses in scripture more beautiful and filled with faithfulness than John's account of the official's response. "The man believed the word that Jesus spoke to him and went his way" (4:50). A song of hope and assurance rang in his heart. His son was going to live. The refrain lingered through the journey.

As the courtier neared his home, he was met by his servants. He could tell at a distance that his fondest wish was true. When they blurted out the triumphant good news that his son was well, he was not surprised. With excitement, he inquired the hour when the fever had subsided. The same faith he had felt when he looked into the face of Jesus pulsed in his being when the servants said, "Yesterday at the seventh hour the fever left him" (John 4:52). One o'clock in the afternoon. A thoughtful, faraway look came over his face. He was thinking about the Master. The very hour Jesus had spoken the word that the man's son would be well, the lad was healed. Gratitude beyond expression filled his heart. And then, an irrepressible desire to see his healed boy!

In this book about the Spirit's fruit, we have dared

to claim a magnificent mind-reorienting future-changing truth. Peter stated it in his second letter: We are "partakers of the divine nature" (2 Peter 1:4). We are saying that to be a Christian is not only to believe in Chirst and try to follow him. It also means that the attributes of his nature are created in us to be manifested through our personalities. What I need every hour and what some of you may need as you read this—more than you need to take your next breath—is the knowledge that God is faithful, and that he can give us faith to trust him.

The fruit of the Spirit is faithfulness.

The psalmist was given an insight into the quality of this kind of faith in the midst of his own tumultuous life marked by ups and downs, successes and failures, battles won and battles lost. The dramatic contrast of his own failure and frustration and the experience of God's timely interventions prompted this explosive praise, "Praise the Lord, all nations! Extol him, all peoples! For great is his steadfast love toward us; and the faithfulness of the Lord endures for ever. Praise the Lord!" (Psalm 117:1-2).

Do you see what the psalmist is doing? He is focusing our need for faithfulness on the very nature of God, and the nature of God's faithfulness is rooted in his steadfast love.

The steadfast nature of the Lord is like an anchor that never pulls off the bottom. It stabilizes the ship in the midst of the storm. It is because God loves us that we know he is faithful. He cannot contradict his own nature. He is unmerited, unchanging, unmotivated love.

The fruit of faithfulness is a result. Faith is a primary gift of the Holy Spirit. It is the imputed gift by which we respond to what God has done for us in Jesus

Christ. "No one can say 'Jesus is Lord' except by the Holy Spirit" (1 Corinthians 12:3). Belief is not our accomplishment. The same God who is creator and sustainer of all, who dwelt in Jesus Christ for the reconciliation of the world, is the same Lord who comes to each of us to give us the capacity to claim what was done for us as the basis of our hope, now and forever. That faith leads to faithfulness, a full-grown faith which dares to believe that all things are possible. It develops as a consistency in all of life. Our faithfulness is not our human follow-through, but our trust that God will follow through in all of life's changes and challenges.

Faithfulness is living expectantly on the amazing resources of God. That means prayer. Since most of our needs have to do with people, it means intercessory prayer. The fruit of faithfulness is expressed in consistent prayer for the faithfulness of God to invade and intercede in the needs of those around us. That is the reason I have focused this chapter on faithfulness in the account of Jesus' miracle of healing of the courtier's son.

John has given us a miracle with profound meaning, an incident bursting with implications for us. Each time the apostle recorded one of the miracles, he told us what happened and then pressed us to wonder about the deeper meaning of what can happen to us.

This is the miracle of intercessory prayer. We see the potential of bringing our concerns for people we love to the Master. The account has several crucial things to say to us about faithfulness in prayer for the sickness, suffering, and supplications of the people of our lives.

This miracle will have its intended impact on us if, as we consider its meaning, each of us focuses on people in need for whom we worry and feel deep anxiety. Most of us have loved ones in our families, among our friends, and in our circle of influence who weigh heavily on our hearts. How shall we pray? Does prayer make any difference? If God knows about their needs, how will our fleeting intercession make any difference?

The first thing this delightful account tells us is that the medium is the first part of a miracle. Some years ago, Marshall McLuhan became famous for his advertising phrase, "The medium is the message." In the case of this miracle, the medium of healing between the Master and the child was the expectant, persistent father who would not leave anything unattempted or untried to get to Jesus and present his need. It was in response to his amazing pertinacity that Jesus healed the sick, fevered child.

We are struck with wonder. The account really teaches that there are some things God will not do until we ask in faith-filled, intercessory prayer.

Note the progression. The man came to Jesus. Pride and self-sufficiency were cast aside. The man surrendered his need completely. He trusted the Lord unreservedly. And he returned home with confident trust.

That is the quality of faith the Lord needs among courageous, praying Christians today. E. Stanley Jones put it directly.

> Prayer does not pull God to us, it pulls us to God. It aligns our wills with his will, so that He can do things through us that He would not otherwise have been able to do. . . . If God has left certain things open in the universe around us to the contingency of man's will—things which will not be done unless man acts—is it strange that He has left certain things open, contingent upon prayer—things which

will never be done unless we do them through prayer?

Prayer is faithfulness in action, pressing through the crowd to place the need before the Master. Intercessory prayer is love and imagination reaching their highest and widest dimensions. And the Lord is always ready to respond. In fact, he has motivated the prayer, and he is more ready to answer than we are to ask.

The Lord's intense longing to bless seems to be graciously limited by his dependence on our intercessory prayers. His love flows freely in response to people who pray for others. Intercessory prayer is the highest expression of love, of a readiness to receive and yield to the working of God's mighty power. We are called to be cooperative agents in the accomplishment of the Lord's purposes. And the miracles the Lord wants to perform around us begin within us, giving us the boldness to come to him about people and their problems and perplexities. Here is the stupendous mystery and the absolute certainty: God waits to act until we pray confident, loving prayers of intercession.

Listen to Jesus as he gives us our royal and holy calling. "If you abide in me, and my words abide in you, ask whatever you will, and it shall be done for you" (John 15:7). "But wait," we say, "That kind of faith is beyond me." No easy escape. The Lord says, "If you have faith as a grain of mustard seed, you will say to this mountain, 'Move hence to yonder place,' and it will move; and nothing will be impossible to you" (Matthew 17:20-21). The words engender faith. We want to dare to be the medium of the miracle.

And yet, a question lingers . . . and then rumbles: Why, knowing the promises of power in response to

intercessory prayer, do we pray so furtively and faith-
lessly—if at all? Perhaps the reason is that we have never
grappled with the law of the universe that intercessory
prayers are an essential part of the unleashing of the
faithfulness of our Lord. Or perhaps we believe in the
power of evil more than the power of the Holy Spirit. We
fear being totally discouraged if we pray and things do
not work out as we had hoped. So we pray seldom, expect little, and are rewarded with even less.

Jesus Christ came to tell us that God loves to bless
his people. "It is your Father's good pleasure to give you
the kingdom," he said (Luke 12:32). But the kingdom is
his rule and authority. Intercessory prayer is seeking and
surrendering to the will of God in the life of a person.
The miracle in us as the medium of prayer power is total
relinquishment. God knows what is best for the people
we love.

Long before Jesus performed the miracle at 1:00
P.M. that afternoon, the miracle of faith had been engendered in the boy's father. That challenges us to pre-
cede our intercessory prayers by taking prolonged time in
prayer with the Lord. Seek him before you seek the
answer to the prayer of intercession. Abide in his presence. Ask for the gift of faith and the knowledge of how
to pray. The miracle will begin with you!

The second thing this exciting account of the healing of the nobleman's son communicates is that there is
no distance in the power of faithful prayer. Jesus did not
have to go to the fevered lad to heal him. This was a
portent and prelude to his ubiquitous, omnipresent ministry as the ascended Lord, unloosed on the world
through the power of the Holy Spirit.

This tells us several things. Only once did Jesus call
his mighty acts miracles. He consistently referred to them

as the works of God. "Truly, truly, I say to you, the Son can do nothing of his own accord, but only what he sees the Father doing" (John 5:19). "The works which the Father has granted me to accomplish, these very works which I am doing, bear me witness that the Father has sent me" (John 5:36). Later in his ministry, Jesus again underlined the fact that what he did was a result of the unlimited power of God in him. On the night before he was crucified, he said, "Do you not believe that I am in the Father and the Father in Me? The words that I say to you I do not speak on my own authority; but the Father who dwells in me does his works" (John 14:10). The amazing resources of God were released through him. He did not have to be physically present at the healing of the nobleman's son because it was the omnipresent power of God that was released at his command.

The same is true today. The name of Jesus releases the same power that healed the lad. "Truly, truly, I say to you, he who believes in me will also do the works that I do; and greater works than these will he do, because I go to the Father" (John 14:12). Jesus had to leave us so that he could return in the power of the Holy Spirit. A lovely description of the Holy Spirit is "Jesus' other self." The promise for our prayers becomes very exciting. "Whatever you ask in my name, I will do it" (John 14:13). And that is true for you and me for our intercessions today. Christ is alive. "In that day you will know that I am in my Father, and you in me, and I in you" (John 14:20). What that means is that we will be guided on how to pray and then be enabled to pray with assurance for others. The same power exposed in the Messiah will flow through our prayers to other people.

Distance makes no difference for the prayer of faith. Neither geographical nor psychological distance is of any consequence. Often, we are separated from people we love; some live at great distances and others with whom we are present are castled in the citadels of their own aloneness which is difficult to penetrate. But we can pray and know that God is at work. We can participate with him in the release of his amazing resources if we will pray.

I want to establish a new word for our faithfulness, *theotelepathy*. It is a combination of *telepathy* and *theopathy*. Telepathy is the communication of one mind with another at a distance by other than sensory means. Contact beyond the physical senses of sight, touch, and hearing of proximity. *Tele* means "distance." *Pathy* from the root of the Greek *paschein*, "passion," meaning to suffer or feel deeply for, or on behalf of another. *Sympathy* and *empathy* come from this stem. Theopathy, on the other hand, is spiritual emotion aroused by meditation on God, prayer. We feel God's love, passion, and suffering concern. *Theo* means "God" in Greek. A theotelepathy, then, is the experience of the love of God engendered by him for another person at a distance. We can reach the needs of others by communication with God, who is more passionately concerned than we are. Evelyn Underhill, the great Christian mystic, once said that through power and love, one human spirit can touch another human spirit. It can take the soul and lift it into the atmosphere of God. People in need of help will find that the person who prays is a transmitter of the redeeming power of God. There is actually a mysterious interpenetration of all living souls.

We have all had the experience of having a person on our mind, only to discover later that that person thought of us at the same time. Also, we have had times when a concern or alarm stirs within us at the very time another person is in great need, danger, or trouble. This is telepathy, the communication of living souls. Faithfulness in prayer raises this to the level of theotelepathy, communication with another through the channel of prayer with God. There is no limitation of distance. The Lord has ordained intercessory prayer as the release of his miraculous power in the life of another, regardless of where he or she is, near or far.

Concern for another person is a message from God that he's ready to work in that person's life if we will cooperate with intercessory prayer. The person's prayers for himself or herself are not enough. God made it that way. God is the initiator of our desire to pray because he wants to reproduce his love in us for the person.

Authentic intercession is rewarded by the "Go your way, your son lives" kind of assurance that Jesus gave to the courtier. That takes relinquishment. We are to pray once and thank God repeatedly that he has heard and that he will answer according to his will and the *ultimate* good of the person for whom we have prayed. It is also a gift of God to "go our way," leaving in God's hands the matter we have prayed about earnestly. To continue to worry after we have interceded is a sure sign that we have not surrendered the need and are still carrying it ourselves for another person. This is lack of faith that the Lord has heard and is active to answer the concern he has placed on our hearts.

This leads to the final thing I want to say. The disciples asked the Lord to teach them to pray. Ours is the same plea. We do not know how to pray for a person in need. What is best in God's strategy for that person?

There are two passages in Paul's letters which help us. The second chapter of 1 Corinthians and chapter one of Ephesians. One tells us of the source of wisdom for our intercessory prayers, and the second gives us the substance of our prayers.

Paul builds his convictions on the source of wisdom from Isaiah 64:4 and 65:17. "What no eye has seen, nor ear heard, nor the heart of man conceived, what God has prepared for those who love him" (Paul's quote of Isaiah in 1 Corinthians 2:9). Then Paul goes on to say that what God has prepared can be revealed to us by the Holy Spirit. "God has revealed [them] to us through the Spirit. For the Spirit searches everything, even the depths of God" (2:10). Only the Spirit knows the cause of the troubles or needs of a person. "What person knows a man's thoughts except the spirit of the man which is in him? So also no one comprehends the thoughts of God except the Spirit of God" (2:11).

It follows that if God knows the thoughts of a person, he can communicate them to us. "Now we have received not the spirit of the world, but the Spirit which is from God, that we might understand the gifts bestowed on us by God. And we impart this in words not taught by human wisdom but taught by the Spirit, interpreting spiritual truths to those who possess the Spirit" (1 Corinthians 2:12-13). The climax of Paul's assurance is that a person who is spiritual (that is, filled with the Holy Spirit) is able to appraise all things because such a person is given the mind of Christ. We can be given insight and discernment for our prayers of intercession. The Spirit's gift is to tell us what he is doing in a person and how to pray for what is best for him or her.

Paul utilizes this gift in his prayers for the Ephesians. In chapter one, he tells his beloved friends how and what he is praying for them.

"I do not cease to give thanks for you, remembering you in my prayers, that the God of our Lord Jesus

Christ, the Father of glory, may give you a spirit of wisdom and of revelation in the knowledge of him, having the eyes of your hearts enlightened, that you may know what is the hope to which he has called you, what are the riches of his glorious inheritance in the saints, and what is the immeasurable greatness of his power in us who believe, according to the working of his great might which he accomplished in Christ when he raised him from the dead" (Ephesians 1:16-20).

This is the mighty charter for our faithful intercessory prayers. It gives us an outline and an inventory of how to pray for others.

1. *Thanksgiving.* We are to praise God for the person for whom we pray and the privilege of being called to a ministry of intercession for him or her.

2. *Pray for the knowledge of God.* Our essential prayer is that people come to know Christ as Savior, Lord, and indwelling power. If a person does not know the Lord, prayer begins with the urgent supplication that whatever he or she is going through will bring him or her to complete trust of the present and the future. So often we pray for solutions before salvation. God may have checkmated people in an impossible situation so that they may discover his love and power.

3. *Pray for wisdom.* Our deepest concern is that whatever is needed in a person's life might bring that person into close communion with God. Wisdom gives a person the capacity to understand the *meaning of the malady.* Today, through medical practice, people can get well before they know the meaning of their sickness,

or they can sublimate a problem before they discover the power of God. Wisdom is given us to pray that people will see the deeper need in their needs: the need for God himself. The one great need above all needs is to give our lives to God.

4. *Pray next for hope.* The eyes of a person's heart need to be enlightened to see that they belong to God, that death has been defeated, and that his Spirit is available to the called and chosen of God for them to face and conquer. As God's person, the one we pray for is a recipient of the inheritance of the saints.

5. *Pray for power.* Paul says that the surpassing greatness of God's power can be given to those who believe. Strength, resurrection, resiliency, the fullness of the Holy Spirit is available. So often people who believe in Christ do not have the intimacy and immediacy of the Spirit. Listen to Jesus, "If you then, who are evil, know how to give good gifts to your children, how much more will your Father who is in heaven give good things to those who ask Him?" (Matthew 7:11). God longs to give himself. The same Spirit who created all, redeemed all in Christ's death and resurrection, is impinging on the one we love. The very problem about which we pray is a secondary need in preparation for the primary need of the Holy Spirit to be met.

6. The last element of praying for another is inherent in Paul's whole epistle: He told them he was praying. *Tell a person for whom you are praying.* Call, write, communicate that you are interceding daily. That may present the oppor-

tunity to talk further about the Lord and his amazing resources.

Now with the special gift of imagination, picture yourself approaching the crowd around Jesus. You long to get through to him about someone you love. Now see the crowd part and the open corridor directly to the Lord made for you. He is there for you. Now stand before him face to face, heart to heart. He is waiting for you to ask for what he is ready to give. Tell him about a person or persons on your heart. Then wait for his answer. At this very moment you prayed, says Jesus, my power has been released in the person for whom you interceded. My will shall be done, in my timing, according to my plan, and for the now and forever blessing of your loved one. You and I are of one heart now. We both love and care. Now go your way in faithfulness.

11
In God's Name, Be Gentle

THERE IS A stereotype for meekness in our culture that is anything but attractive. It is a Milquetoast kind of person whose only vocal contribution is the sound of the throat being cleared for speech that never comes.

If you have bought this stereotype, it may come as a distinct shock to you to know that meekness or gentleness is a characteristic of God that the Spirit has implanted and wants to develop in you. God wants to make us his meek and gentle people in the midst of history.

In Paul's inventory of the fruit of the Spirit, the King James Version translates this quality as meekness, but it means something quite different from the weakness the word has been associated with. *Gentleness* is a far better word. It is an essential part of God's fatherly grace which he wants modeled by us, his own children.

There is a marvelous story I remember hearing about Alexander the Great. A child he had sired grew to manhood and joined his father's army. In one of the battles he was exposed for his fear and was brought before the commanding general. Alexander did not recognize his own son. The demands of a military life had kept him from association with the boy as he grew. He did know, however, that he was looking into the face of a coward. The charge was justified. The account was true.

Alexander looked him squarely in the eye and said, "Young man, what is your name?"

"A . . . Al . . . Alexander, sir," the boy stuttered.

Alexander the Great said a second time, "Young man, what is your name?"

"A . . . Al . . . Alexander, sir," was the response. And then, reviewing the young man's cowardly act, Alexander took him by the shoulders and shook him and said, "Change your character, or change your name!"

There is an inescapable message here for us. If we call ourselves Christians, we need to have the character imprint of God and his Son upon us. We need to change our character—or change our name.

The fruit of the Spirit is gentleness.

I was forcibly reminded of that one day when a chain of highly irritating—and in my mind grossly unnecessary—mechanical problems immobilized my car on the corner of Gower Street and Sunset Boulevard. Already behind for an appointment, I called the auto club. Two hours and not one but two auto club trucks later, my car finally started. I was in a turbulent mood as I headed back up Gower Street on my way to Glendale for my belated speaking engagement. I was thinking of all the ways I could express my frustration in a letter to the president of the auto club, when I caught a glimpse of the marquee of my own church announcing the next

Sunday's sermon title the Lord had guided a whole year before: "In God's Name, Be Gentle!" I needed the admonition more than the people who would hear the sermon on gentleness. But then, God often gives me a fresh experience of what I am planning to preach.

There is no other way to be gentle than by the name and power the Lord gives us. Authentic gentleness is one of the most miraculous manifestations of the inner splendor of Christ's indwelling. It requires absolute trust in his ongoing work in others. It responds to the wonder of what people have been through, not what they have done. It addresses the emerging child, often hurt and battered, in other people.

The Lord is consistently gentle with us. He stands beside us in the midst of trouble and tragedy, nursing us through it all. That is the same kind of encouragement the people around us need.

What does it mean to be gentle in life's tensions and problems? It certainly does not mean simply having a moldable, adjustable, easy lack of concern. Moses was referred to as one of the meekest men in all of Israel, and yet he martialed the mass exodus of a diverse company of people and brought them through the wilderness to the promised land.

But it is in Jesus Christ that we see gentleness in its true light. Though the word is not used, the passage which shows us true gentleness is the account of the Passover feast in the thirteenth chapter of John's Gospel. "Jesus, knowing that the Father had given all things into his hands, and that he had come from God and was going to God rose from supper, laid aside his garments, and girded himself with a towel. Then He poured water into a basin, and began to wash the disciples' feet" (John 13:3-5). Jesus knew who he was and what he had come to do. He could do the servant's work. His life and death portrays gentleness. He loved his enemies and followers alike, those who deceived him, betrayed him, and crucified him. He was totally free of defensiveness.

The same character that was in Christ shall be in us. I wonder if that is the reason the French in the translation of this beatitude, "Blessed are the meek . . .," used the word *debonaire*. For the French that means winsome and free because you know the source of your power.

But let's press on. The word *praotēs* from *praus* in Greek has a profound implication for us. For Aristotle it stood for the mean point between too much anger and too little anger, a point between over-expression and under-expression. A meek or gentle person was one who was under such control that he or she was able to express the reality of each emotion without excess.

There is more. The word *praus,* as I mentioned earlier, describes an animal which has been brought under the reins or control of a master and is now guidable. The truly meek are those who have gone through an experience when their arrogant self-will has been broken. They have come to a place of deep humility. *Praus* in Greek is the opposite of *hyperēphania*. Pride is always contrasted with humility. It is holding oneself above others instead of caring for others under the control of the Master's reins.

When we are truly meek, we know who we are because we know to whom we belong. We do not have to be defensive or justify ourselves any longer. We know we are loved and are therefore free to love and free to be the unique, special, unreproduceable wonders that God meant us to be. Once the defensive pride is taken from us by an authentic experience of humility, we are able to treat others like God has treated us.

I was fascinated as I studied the word *meekness* (or *gentleness*) in many different biblical settings and found it to be a relational word. It deals with the correction of one Christian by another and how to treat persons in the midst of problems.

After Paul has listed the fruit or characteristics of the Spirit to the Galatians, he is quoted in the sixth chapter as saying: "Brethren, if a man is overtaken in any trespass, you who are spiritual should restore him in a spirit of gentleness. Look to yourself, lest you too be tempted" (6:1). It is out of a recognition of our own inadequacy that we can be tender toward others.

I read a newspaper account of a speech reportedly given by Madalyn Murray O'Hair. Her audience of young people listened patiently as she gave her speech opposing religion in American life and her deprecation of God and faith. When she concluded, a young woman stood up and spoke with gentle purpose. She thanked Ms. O'Hair for coming to speak and told her that the young people had listened with attention. Then she told her that she thanked her for showing them what an atheist really is. She expressed gratitude to her for strengthening their beliefs by her attack. Then she told her how sorry they were for her. Again she thanked her for coming and said they had even more love and faith in God as a result of seeing what life without God would be.

Now that is meekness in defense of the faith, meekness that has strength. In the deafening applause that followed the girl's words, Ms. O'Hair left the platform.

Meekness should be the basis of receiving the word of God. James says, "Therefore put away all filthiness and rank growth of wickedness and receive with meekness the implanted word, which is able to save your souls" (James 1:21).

129

James has given us the secret in the word *receive.*
True meekness or gentleness is receptivity. We cannot
give away what we have not received. Nor can we receive all that God wants to give us unless we give away
what is given to us for others. This is the magnificent
meaning of the third beatitude. The gentle inherit the
earth. They are the blessed. Note the progression in the
beatitude. Blessed means beloved, belonging to God,
cherished, called, and chosen. Those who know their
sublime status are able to be gentle, completely open to
what God wants to give and sensitive to his guidance.
Because they are, they can inherit the earth. The phrase
has its roots in Psalm 37:11, "But the meek shall possess
the land, and delight themselves in abundant prosper-
ity." To the Hebrews it meant first the promised land,
then the providence of God, and finally the fulfillment
of the Messianic age. Surely the latter was on Jesus' mind
when he gave this secret of blessedness. All that he had
come to be and do would be available to those who were
receptive. His nature would be implanted and his power
unleashed in them. Paul underlined this when he called
us "joint-heirs with Christ." Our inheritance was sealed
on Calvary, assured on Easter, and completed on Pentecost. Meekness is being open to the new and fresh thing
God wants to give so that we can become channels of his
grace to others.

Now look at the results. Catch the power and sig-
nificance if you will. The meek shall eat and be satisfied.
Jesus will guide the meek in judgment. He will teach
them his way.

We inherit the earth because we are children of the
Father, and everything that is his belongs to us. When
his nature is in us, we become free to be gentle, free to
love because our Father's love has built a rock at the core

of our personalities. We know we are God's children and are free to be that with abandonment. "See what love the Father has given us, that we should be called children of God; and so we are. Beloved, we are God's children now; it does not yet appear what we shall be, but we know that when he appears we shall be like him, for we shall see him as he is" (1 John 3:1-2).

Far from being apologetic in manner, God's gentleness that we inherit is a mind-set that shapes and tempers the style of what we are as the people of God. Now on the basis of all that, we can allow the Lord to cure our future worries. Activate the characteristic of gentleness implicit in your new heredity. Become a gracious receiver. I suspect that what God has done in the past is nothing in comparison with what he is ready to do. Now. Today. Trust him.

The only time the future tense is used in a salutation or greeting in the epistles of the New Testament is in the second letter of John. He says: "Grace, mercy, and peace will be with us." That's the assurance I need. We are rooted in the very nature of God, in his plan for us, the way he works with us, and what happens inside us.

Gentleness is the key given to us to trust what God did in Jesus Christ as our Savior. That is a gift. And gentleness is also a spiritual muscle inherent in our new nature, waiting to be exercised to unlock the resources of the power of God to apply to our specific situations. Only that kind of inner strength is an antidote to anxiety. Only faith can cure our lack of trust. And as the nature of God begins to grow in us, we become identifiably gentle people.

How many people can you count on, really count on, to share the vision and the adventure? How many people are rocklike points of reference in your life?

I have a friend who calls me whenever he is alerted by God to the fact that I need a particular touch of grace. "Lloyd, I'm with you all the way!" he will say. And he has done that for thirty-five years!

So many of us are like mercury where our faith is concerned, so hesitant to connect our character to God's consistency. I know because I am often like that myself. Not long ago I found myself at the intersection of the payment of a horrendous tax bill and the fulfillment of a mission pledge. I looked at my checkbook and all of my assets and it was obvious I could not pay both of them. I was about to leave for a tour of our missionaries in the Orient, and I knew it would be hard to present myself as someone firmly behind missions if I had not paid my own pledge.

I went through the whole day with some uneasiness about the matter before I had time to open my folder of mail in my study. There was a check in that folder from a publisher for an amount I had not anticipated receiving. I did not know whether to laugh or cry so I did both. It was for the exact amount I needed.

God is faithful. Because he is, we can be the gentle, meek people of the world. We can trust our future to him.

12
Call Central Casting
for the Real You

THE MOVIE COMPANIES in Hollywood have special departments called central casting. They coordinate the selection of actors and actresses for parts in movie productions. "Call central casting" is a familiar refrain of directors and producers when someone is needed for a particular part.

The other day, I visited a movie set where one of my members was taking part in a scene of a forthcoming movie. While sitting on the sideline watching with great interest, I overheard a fascinating conversation.

A young actor came on the set to do a bit part. The director looked at him, sizing him up for the drama. "Who are you?" he asked insistently. The young man gave his name. "I don't want your name, but the part you're playing!" the director replied. The befuddled fledgling was not sure. I'll never forget the director's impatient response. "You'd better call central casting and find out who you are!"

You are probably ahead of me about the parable I got out of that exchange. Add a definite article to the director's command and you really have something. Call *the* central casting and find out who you are. In the drama of real life our greatest challenge is to know who we are and be faithful to that person in every way. Only the ultimate casting director, the Lord himself, can help us with that.

Each of us is a unique, never-to-be-repeated miracle. So often we deny that uniqueness by trying to contradict the real person we are inside. I think e. e. cummings was right. Being yourself in a world where everyone is trying to make you somebody else is the hardest battle a human being can fight.

The last of the fruit of the Spirit gives us power to do just that. Self-control, the final jewel of the inner splendor mentioned under Paul's code name *fruit*, is the one which makes all the rest operative. To the Greek, self-control was to have "power over oneself." Paul grasped this quality from the four cardinal virtues of the Stoics and claimed it as one of the imputed vibrancies of the Holy Spirit. The Greek word, *egkrateia*, from the ancient root *egratēs*, means holding control. It is often translated as temperance, as in the King James Version of the Bible. But since temperance is often used in a very limited sense, I much prefer the broader and deeper implications of self-control.

This sublime fruit of the Spirit is not negative. It does not delineate what we are against or will not do. Rather it consists of a very positive capacity to know who we are and what we will do because the Spirit is in control of our abilities and aptitudes, as well as our appetites. We can have power over ourselves only when we have submitted to the Spirit's control and power *in* us. Christ control is the basis of self-control. Call *the* central casting, the Lord himself, for the real you.

Self-control is inseparably related to the fruit of gentleness. In the previous chapter we discovered that means living with the knowledge that Christ is in us. Such an awareness results in the development of the special person each of us was created to be. It is very exciting to realize that our Lord has a strategy and plan for each of us.

We often think of personality as the irrevocable result of parental and environmental conditioning. A young man said to his father, "What I am is what you've made me. The ship has come in." That is to evade the opportunity and responsibility we all have of the Lord's reshaping of our personalities. He can affirm and strengthen what we are that is in keeping with the uniqueness he planned for us, and then he can reform anything that distorts or hinders our becoming all that we were meant to be. When we yield our personalities to his scrutiny and renovation, he begins a magnificent transformation. That means surrendering our values, attitudes, actions, and reactions to him. In profound times of prayer meditation, we can talk to him about the person we are in every dimension and relationship and then listen to him as he tenderly shows us areas that need to be remolded to be more like him. The secret of discovering a truly unique personality is to focus on Christ. We become like our heros. He is the only reliable hero of our souls. The better we know him, the more we concentrate on his message and life, the closer we will come to being the special, distinct persons he intended. It is amazing. The deeper we grow in Christ, the more we become free to be our true selves. He does not put us into a straitjacket of sameness. Rather, he liberates us with new values, priorities, attitudes, and goals which begin to surface in our personalities. Human nature can be changed. We do not have to remain the people we are.

Recently, I have experienced great physical reformation in intensive physiotherapy. In a series of ten sessions with a highly trained physiotherapist, my body has undergone remarkable changes. Tightened tendons, conditioned by years of bad habits of posture and relating to my body, have been stretched and released. A hump in my back, formed by long hours slouched over my writing desk, has been removed. Constricted muscles in my stomach which were pulling me down into a stooped posture have been liberated so that I can stand up straight. Forty-nine years of self-conditioning of my body are being reversed. Over the months of therapy I have grown an inch! I do not have to be the physical person I was for the rest of my life. The body is like plastic and under the skilled hands of the therapist, I have been liberated to stand, walk, and sit differently.

I have shared this personal experience as an illustration that none of us needs to remain the person we are. What that series of treatments did to my body, Christ has done and continues to do with my personality. I am not the personality I was; nor am I the person I will be. Seldom a day goes by without the Lord's impact. Ever since I yielded the control of my personality development to him, he has been at work. He's not finished with me, nor will he ever be. In daily times with him, he helps me look back over what I have been, said, and done. He always begins with what has been creative and good. Then, with masterful sensitivity, he penetrates into my relationships with myself and others. His questions are incisive. "Why did you feel it necessary to do or say that?" "What insecurity, defensiveness, or arrogance caused this?" "What would you have been like if you had been trusting me and my guidance in that situation?" Following that is a remedial time of thinking with him how I can be more his person in the future.

The Lord offers us five *I*'s for discovering the real *I*. The first is *introspection*. That means daring to look inward to discover the roots of our personality. Why are we the people we are? What shaped our character? Whom are we trying to emulate? What is right and what is less than maximum?

The second step is *integration*. Christ gives us the inner control over our persons. When we put him first in our lives, seek first his kingdom, and want what he wants for us, there is a new integration around his lordship. This is the control that liberates. Memories are sorted out, values are scrutinized, hopes are refashioned.

The third flows naturally. From integration comes *integrity*. We can dare to be outwardly what the Lord has enabled us to be inwardly. Integrity is the capacity to act in keeping with our beliefs and convictions—consistency! People around us will be able to say those seven dynamic words we all long to hear: "What you see is what you get." We all want to be people on whom others can depend in life's changes and challenges. We urgently desire to be the kind of parents, friends, leaders whose attitudes and actions will be predictably consistent with the individual persons we really are.

Intuition is the fourth dimension. A life under Christ's control is gifted with an inner device that discerns the right and does it. The Spirit's gifts of wisdom and discernment give us X-ray vision to see beneath the surface of things. We are empowered to think clearly

137

and feel sensitively about what is going on around us. The mind and emotions become agents of the Spirit to guide us in times of pressure and opportunity. I have a friend who has yielded to the Spirit's control so completely that he can penetrate deeply into problems and see the potential for advancement they offer. People around him are often heard to remark, "That guy sees and understands. How come his perception is so sharp?" The fruit of self-control as a result of Christ control is the only explanation. His faithfulness to daily prayer makes him an effective, intuitive leader. It is a supernatural gift. Without the Holy Spirit he would be as dull, insensitive, and unadventuresome as the people whom he constantly amazes.

The final "I" is *individuality*. We hear a lot of I've-got-to-be-me! individualism which is a poor facsimile for Christ-centered individuality. Individualism is a self-conscious effort to be different and distinct. It always calls attention to itself and must be fortified by disclaimers such as "Well, that's who I am. If you don't like it, that's your problem!" Individuality is inadvertent. The focus is on Christ and not on ourselves. We do not need to bother to be different. Christ is our difference. He makes us individuals free to live by grace and follow his guidance. The result will be a person unlike anyone else and yet one who is concerned more about others than ourselves. The old statement, "God threw away the mold after he made him" is both true and untrue. Our mold is Christ and we come back to him repeatedly for the clay of our personalities to be recast. The result will be freedom from self-consciousness or defensiveness.

In the context of all this we can take another look at the word temperance as a translation of *egkrateia*. A tempered person has gone through the refining process.

He or she has been hammered out on the anvil of the Lord's gracious but persistent reshaping. Then temperance is freedom from eccentric extremes and indulgences. The things which do not contribute to the Lord's best for us can be discarded or used without compulsion. Nothing that we eat or drink will be needed to fortify a depleted ego. Behavior patterns which trip us up in following Christ can be faced and surrendered to him. All the things we consume or the distracting habits we form out of intemperance will be dislodged from their hold on us.

There is a great word called *equipoise.* It means balance. When the inner power of Christ is balanced perfectly with the outward pressures of the world, that is equipoise. It is another way of describing self-control.

We live in such a beguiling world. As we are pulled in so many directions it is easy to allow our minds to drift into fantasies, our wills to make decisions which are not consistent with the character of Christ, and our bodies to be engaged in practices which are not in keeping with his lordship.

Everything that was manifest in the character of Jesus of Nazareth is reproducible in you and me. "The Father and I will come and make our home in you," Christ said. It is a word of cheer and a word of challenge.

Paul gives the Galatians, and us, the secret of how to realize power over oneself. He says that we have crucified the flesh, and now as we live by the Spirit we should also walk by the Spirit. "The Spirit has given us life; he must also control our lives" (Galatians 5:25, TEV).

The term *flesh* is a kind of biblical shorthand for our humanity independent and separate from Jesus Christ. The exciting life begins when our minds, emotions, wills, and bodies are joyously surrendered to Christ's infinite control. That also includes every relationship of our lives. When we walk in the Spirit, Paul says, we will not fulfill the lusts of the flesh.

Do you remember when you took your first steps "in the Spirit?" Just as we learn to commit our weight to the ground step by step, in the same way we reach out to venture love and peace, patience and kindness, beyond our own hoarded resources, confident of the Spirit's limitless and available supply. Soon we have acquired the greatest skill of all—walking in the Spirit.

For Christians battling the pull of the lower nature, Paul's code name *fruit* is an invitation to a radical transformation of the whole of human existence. Paul lists the "works of the flesh" in Galatians 5 and heralds the fruit of the Spirit as the antidote. For example, when we go around nursing giant-size hostilities, initiating quarrels, and constantly putting up opposite points of view, we are boycotting the Spirit's stores of gentleness and peace.

When we are fully in touch with who we are—the new persons we are in Christ—an unmistakable outward radiance will reflect the splendor within. We have discovered the thermostatic control that opens the channel to becoming the new breed of men and women we were intended to be. There is no way to hide it.

A year ago I had a wonderful period of uninterrupted time with my mother. She is eighty-three years old. Mother had a new red dress made for the occasion, spent the morning at the hairdressers, cleaned the house, had the coffee on the stove, and was all ready for my arrival.

We sat and talked like we had not talked for years, and like we might never talk again. She got out some of the old scrapbooks and albums, and entrusted to me a photo that is now one of my most cherished possessions. It was a picture of my father when he was my age. Years before she had put it away to give to me in such a moment. My eyes devoured the photo for marks of the heredity we shared. I traced the lines and contours in my father's face now evident in my own.

I trust the same kind of excitement has been in you as you have read these chapters. Have you been looking for and detecting the inescapable marks of an emerging family likeness to your own heredity? Paul's code name *fruit*, far from being archaic, is the flash of an eloquent symbol to remind us that all the graces and characteristics of God are to be modeled in the daily life and relationships of his children.

Are we doing it? Are we giving the world a symmetrical, authentic, fully-formed image of Christ? There is still time. Spiritual growth is not a matter of chronology alone. It's a matter of spirit. Of heart. Of who you are to the next person you meet. In the next crisis you face. In the next moment you live.

Central casting is calling. There is a need for someone to be the real you. Why not you? The radiance of the inner splendor eminently qualifies you to take the part.

About the Author

LLOYD JOHN OGILVIE attended Lake Forest College, Garrett Theological Seminary, and New College, Faculty of Theology, University of Edinburgh during his studies for the ministry.

Dr. Ogilvie is the pastor of First Presbyterian Church, Hollywood, California. He serves as a member of numerous community organizations and ministerial associations in Hollywood. Before going to First Presbyterian, Dr. Ogilvie served pastorates in Illinois and Pennsylvania.

Each of the churches Dr. Ogilvie has served has been a laboratory of experimentation with new forms of church life and innovative methods of training the laity for ministry. Using the relational approach to the gospel, Dr. Ogilvie stresses four basic relationships—with God, oneself, others, and the world. Through a program of renewal conferences, small groups, and lay training, beginning first with church officers and then throughout the congregation, church members are discovering a vital faith and an involvement in social issues and concerns. A seminary for the laity, called the Laos Academy, is also part of the equipping ministry.

Dr. Ogilvie appears weekly on the nationally syndicated television program, "Let God Love You!" The program seeks to help people turn their struggles into stepping-stones. Dr. Ogilvie is frequently a spiritual leader and speaker at conferences, universities, and local churches and is the author of numerous books.